MW00366502

# *Serendib*

# Serendib

JIM TONER

THE UNIVERSITY OF GEORGIA PRESS

ATHENS AND LONDON

Paperback edition published in 2013 by
The University of Georgia Press
Athens, Georgia 30602
www.ugapress.org
© 2001 by Jim Toner
All rights reserved
Designed by Erin Kirk New
Set in 12 on 14 Centaur

Printed digitally

The Library of Congress has cataloged the hardcover
edition of this book as follows:
Toner, Jim, 1956–
Serendib / Jim Toner.
216 p. ; 22 cm.
ISBN 0-8203-2269-5 (alk. paper)
1. Toner, John, 1915– —Travel—Sri Lanka.
2. Sri Lanka—Description and travel. I. Title.
DS489.T65    2001
915.49304'32—dc21
00-044724

Paperback ISBN-13: 978-0-8203-4661-8
ISBN-10: 0-8203-4661-6

British Library Cataloging-in-Publication Data available

# *Acknowledgments*

Many people helped me over the last nine years to bring this story to you. Above all, I thank my father, whose brave visit to Sri Lanka gave me a story I had to write—and so much more. As for the writing itself, I pay special thanks to the sanctuary and community of the Vermont Studio Center; to Musa Mayer and Jerry Meyer, who slogged through the early drafts with me; to my parents, who never looked sideways at me when I lived with them for free and drove a cab so I could work on this book; to the kind ladies on the third floor of the old Cleveland Library; to Malcolm Call and Stephen Barnett; and to Joe and George, Moi and Christian, Peter and Vonna and Anthony. Finally, there are two women who deserve special notice: to Sue Silverman, who wouldn't rest until this story found its way out into the world; and to Dolora, my wife and best friend, who has turned every step of my life into joy and play and serendipity.

For my parents,

John and Lillie Ann,

and for

my brothers,

Joe and George

Where we had thought to find an abomination,
we shall find a god. And where we had thought
to slay another, we shall slay ourselves. Where we
had thought to travel outward, we will come to the
center of our own existence. And where we had
thought to be alone, we will be with all the world.

JOSEPH CAMPBELL

*Serendib*

I didn't invite him.

The idea was all my father's, my seventy-four-year-old father who had never been outside America and who suddenly thought that Sri Lanka, where I was a Peace Corps volunteer, would be a jolly place to visit. He didn't know where it was, though he'd heard of its former name, Ceylon. He didn't know about the hepatitis and typhoid shots he'd have to get. And he certainly didn't know that its two civil wars gave Sri Lanka, in April 1990, the distinction of being the world's deadliest country.

"You're coming?" I asked him over the phone. "Are you kidding?"

"Kidding? Sounds like a real adventure to me. Monkeys, parrots, all those monk fellows wandering around. Malone, he's been there. He tells me there's elephants strolling the boulevards like shoppers. Say, Jimmy, should I bring a tie?"

"Dad, maybe you ought to—"

"And cobras! No cobras here in Cleveland, Jimmy. Now Malone, he tells me to bring over my Irish flute, conjure those little buggers right out of their holes. How about my Hush Puppies? Think I'll be needing them, or should I just go with the wing tips? I'm figuring a tie doesn't take up much space and well, whadya think, Jimmy?"

My wife Cindy, sitting next to me in the Peace Corps office in the capital city of Colombo, jumped up and clapped. "He's coming? He's really coming?"

I held my hand over the receiver and told her again that I thought the idea was trouble, big trouble. "He's old and he hates heat and the bombs are getting worse, and, God, what could I even say to the guy for—"

"Jimmy? Jimmy, are you still there? Listen, I know the Hush Puppies may not be the most practical choice. But they sure are comfortable as slippers, and my bunions, jeez, they're acting up these days, and so . . ."

And on he went about the miracle of Dr. Scholl's shoe inserts. But I was barely listening. My head was too filled with the preposterous image of my father on Sri Lankan soil, and so after his bunion and corn report I reminded him about how genuinely bleak and violent this place really was: Sure, Dad, come on over and see two civil wars up close. Go get those typhoid shots in your sagging white rump, and then come face-to-face with the malaria and the rabid dogs, the buses without brakes, the suffocating tropical heat. There are wooden beds waiting for your bony hips, Dad, and no English, and no toilet paper, and no forks—but enough snakes to fill up your nightmares. So come. Come where the cockroach is king and murder is sport. Come spend seven hundred uninterrupted hours with the last of your seven kids, the one you vaguely know and who vaguely knows you. For the first time in your life, leave America; for the first time in fifty years, leave your wife. Come, Dad. Come to the other side of the planet. Come to where every one of your demons is waiting to ambush you.

"All I know for sure is this, Jimmy. Wing tips are the safe way to go. Hush Puppies, they're too hot and they show the dirt too easy. Decided. Wing tips it is, wing tips it'll be."

"Dad, that's great. Wing tips'll fit in perfect over here. But listen, I'm just a bit worried that the bombs we hear every night will—"

"Jimmy, we've all got our problems. Jeesh, I'm driving your mother nuts sitting around here all day, and with all this retirement money I thought about Florida. Florida, Sri Lanka—it doesn't matter to your mother. She's just tickled pink to be getting me out of her hair for a bit."

"Save me, Jimmy. Save me now." It was my mom, and I could tell by the sound of *Wheel of Fortune* in the background that she was on the extension in her bedroom. I could picture her clearly, sitting on the edge of the thick mattress with her feet on the plush carpet and her phone balanced on the stack of Danielle Steele romances, all bathed in the eternal blue light of the TV. It sounded like Pat Sajak and all the jolly folks of *Wheel of Fortune* were having the time of their lives, and I thought: Keep it all twelve thousand miles away from me.

"Hi, Mom. How's life in Cleveland?"

"Jimmy, your father's driving me nuts. Get this: He's starting to vacuum. Can you imagine your father with a vacuum? And last night, get this: He decides to cook us dinner. First time in his life. So what does the nut make? Tomato soup. Straight from a can."

"With crackers," my dad said. "Cheese flavored."

"Thinks he's a chef now, the royal nut. Time to get him out of my hair before we both get shipped to the loony barn."

"Cindy," I whispered, "we've got problems."

She told me to stop worrying. "He'll be fine and, God, how amazing. He's really coming!"

My dad told me that the crackers were new from Nabisco. "Cute little cheese-flavored things. Says on the box they're the rage of Paris. Anyhow, just you watch how your mother'll be crying for my cuisine when I'm away with you kids. Now listen, don't you let me upset your life over there. You just keep on working and . . . Hey, what is it you kids do over there, anyhow?"

I rolled my eyes. For the hundredth time over the course of the past two years I repeated, "Teachers, Dad. We're TEACHERS!"

3

"Oh, that's right, Jimmy. Your mother, she's got me all in a muddle over here. Hey, Lil, you still on the phone?"

"No, John. I'm not on the phone."

"That's your mother's humor for you. Anyhow, Jimmy, that'll be some kind of a treat to see you kids up in a classroom. Say, you folks got computers over there? I understand they're all the rage these days."

"Computers? Dad, we don't even have books or enough desks, and the goats keep eating the chalk. And most of the time the schools are shut down, anyway—you know, that little inconvenience of a civil war. You'll be lucky to catch us in action at all."

It was true. We had an official job title as Peace Corps volunteers—"English teachers" to Sri Lankan adults preparing to become teachers—but because of the two civil wars a more accurate job title for us could have been "Lords of Idleness." A teacher would have been frustrated by all of the school closings, but we Lords of Idleness just went home, erased old crossword puzzles, and then redid them again and again until the eraser broke through the paper. A teacher would have gone berserk waiting indoors for the week-long curfews to end; we Lords of Idleness just hunkered down with one of our local library's peculiar English books, as I did with *Blue Eyes: The Biography of Paul Newman* and *Offensive Schemes of the Boston Celtics*. How these books and others like them—*Finnegans Wake*, early issues of *Mad* magazine, all of Agatha Christie, *Woodworking Made Easy*—ever made it to the remote village of Bandarawela, no one ever knew.

"Hey, Dad," I said, "we're really *overjoyed* you're coming here"— Cindy snorted at my lie—"but, you know, are you sure you're up for all these bugs and heat and all that war stuff I've told you about?"

"Aw, heck, Malone tells me—you know Malone, Gus Malone, fella who works at the court? He's been to that Sir Lanker place—"

"'Sri,' Dad. It's 'Sri Lanka.' At least get that much straight."

"Hey, I'm no language expert, okay? Anyhow, Malone's been to that Lanker place at least a dozen times—he's an expert, Jimmy.

An expert. And Malone tells me to just strap on some earplugs and give a ball-point pen to anyone who looks at me sideways. Violence! Come back to Cleveland, Jimmy, and I'll show you some violence."

This was not a good sign. It was bad enough that my dad thought a trip to Sri Lanka would be as exotic and risky as a jaunt across Lake Erie to Detroit. But now he held the delusion that a lifetime in Cleveland had actually prepared him for the savagery of Sri Lanka. Last time I looked there were no suicide bombers in Cleveland detonating themselves on crowded buses or in front of political candidates. No teenage soldiers prowled the streets of Cleveland with rifles slung over their shoulders. Nowhere in all of Ohio were the distant sounds at night of explosions and gunfire so routine that Sri Lankans, and myself, most noticed them when they stopped. And I doubt that anywhere near my parents' condominium, with its manicured lawn and tidy flower beds, was there a circle of thirty-two rebel heads stuck on poles—as there was an hour from my front doorstep in Bandarawela.

Sri Lanka was no Cleveland. Especially in the spring of 1990, this was a country busy destroying itself. In the north and the east, the minority Hindu Tamils were battling the majority Buddhist Sinhalese for a section of the island to call their own. That was an ancient struggle. But out of that remote war sprang a new one in 1987, a more terrifying one that targeted our neighbors, our post office, our buses that we rode every day. This secondary war pitted the Sinhalese against the Sinhalese—specifically, the very corrupt Sinhalese government against the ultranationalist, leftist Sinhalese group, the JVP (Janatha Vimukthi Peramuna, or People's Liberation Front). In its strategy to overthrow the government, the JVP randomly destroyed government property (schools, buses) and randomly assassinated government workers and their families. For a while our village principal roamed the jungle at night, sleeping in a different home each evening. He was lucky to survive; many of the other neighboring principals were killed. So were many of the tea-plantation managers, one of whom Cindy and I had stayed with the weekend before he was shot through the head. "I know how to handle the JVP," he had told us confidently. "They really are gentlemen, and you must treat them like gentlemen."

News of his death hardly fazed Cindy and me, so desensitized had we become from two years of steady violence in Sri Lanka. Still, we shuddered when the green Mitsubishi jeeps rounded up some of our older male students, eventually "disappearing" them; some of the "disappeared" became part of the daily run of corpses floating down rivers. When we saw crowds leaning over bridges, we knew what they were tallying. And we also knew that when we passed smoldering tires by the roadside, what we smelled was more than just burning rubber.

"Dad, believe me," I said over the phone, "you're going to need a lot more than earplugs and pens to survive over here. I'll try to protect you, but you're bound to see some horrific things."

"Malone, he tells me I'll be too busy looking at elephants and waterfalls to notice any trouble."

"Jimmy. Jimmy, this is your mother again. Listen, I know you'll take good care of your father—you're a good boy—but just remember he's got a little bladder problem so help him at night and please keep his salt down, and I'm worried sick he'll forget his Coppertone, oh his skin is so quick to burn. And I've already told him to pick me up one of those blue sapphires like Malone got his wife Peggy. You know, Jimmy, we're all a little bit tired of that Peggy showing off her ring to us like she's Elizabeth Taylor or something."

"Mom," I said, "*what* are you talking about?"

"I'll send you some cookies, Jimmy. I wish I could send you some corned-beef sandwiches, but who can say if they'll stay fresh. You know, your father's tickled pink about seeing a cobra or two. Do they really have cobras over there, honey?"

And that was that. It was too late for me to deter him from coming to a place where he really didn't belong, a place too primitive and too hazardous for anyone's father. He knew all this, and yet what could any of it possibly mean, I thought, to someone protected in an American cocoon for seventy-four years? His was a world of the microwaved potato and the sanitized toilet bowl, of leather recliners and automatic garage-door openers, of air conditioning and cruise control. But maybe, just maybe, he was tired of it all. Maybe he sensed that a lifetime of storm windows and neon-blue bug zappers had kept him disconnected from nature too long. Maybe in coming to Sri Lanka he was questioning whether all those protections had been necessary after all.

But I was speculating. I had no idea who this man was, this Cleveland judge living in an era when, as a good Irish Catholic, his role was to procreate often and work long hours, and then clear out of the way while my mother did the raising. I had no idea what his motives and capacities were, his longings, his thrills, his history. Had he ever ridden a bike? Who was his first date? Did his father take him to baseball games? Who were his friends?

But to be honest, I wasn't interested in any heart-to-heart talks with my dad. Maybe I had become too hardened from living for two years in a country where bombs and terror were part of daily life. Whatever the reason, all I really wanted from my dad on this trip was a box of my mom's chocolate-chip cookies. And maybe one more thing: to swim alongside me in the Indian Ocean.

I craved this swim. The most radiant moment—the *only* radiant moment—I had ever experienced with my father was in the Atlantic Ocean when I was four. It was 1960, and we had just driven ten hours to Ocean City, Maryland, in our green Pontiac filled with one sister and five big brothers, most of whom took turns beating me up. While everyone else unpacked, my father took me and me alone, hand in hand, across the beach and down to the surf. "The ocean, Jimmy," he said, spreading wide his arms. "I give you the ocean."

7

It was dusk, and the waves loomed as high and menacing as storm clouds. I wanted no part of this ocean, frothing and heaving like one of my cartoon monsters, but the hand I held eased me into the ocean. I remember that hand well: the soft hills and deep lines of his palm, the fingers sure as cables. To me, the power of that hand could outmuscle the sea. I tightened my little hand in his and together, through the sea spray, we ran into the ocean and under the waves. I probably gulped salt water and probably cried, but as long as my dad sheltered me in the curve of his chest, I didn't care. I was alone with my father in the sway of the sea. Later, I held onto his back as we rode wave after wave into shore, the two of us skidding to a stop with sand filling our swimsuits. We went back again and again until the dusk turned to night, and finally, holding hands, we returned slowly to a cottage full of other children, all of them wanting their own hands held, all of them eager to teach me the Irish sport of ridiculing my father behind his back.

Too many hands, too much ridicule, too much judge work, and so the years following this one radiant moment alone with my dad in the sea never quite matched up. Except for a few brief moments, I'm not sure I was ever alone with him again. In fact, I'm sure of it, just as I'm sure that I never made him laugh or ever did anything that made him stop and notice me.

Invisible boys like me often grow up to be teachers. I did, and for a while it felt good to at least be noticed by teenage students in California, even if that notice came by force—the force of grades, the force of being trapped in desks. But all along what I really wanted, even though I was a very big boy, was for my dad to turn his attention to me, the teacher. It never happened, and in time I just figured that I would only be truly worthy in his eyes if I were to become either a priest or a lawyer, and the priest option had died long ago from too much reason and too much flesh.

So off to law school I went. For the first month there I studied obsessively, reading and rereading each case a dozen times, typing up neat and concise summaries and analyses with columns and arrows and key words in bold just for that one moment when my professor would call on me. One night he did. I stood, and I realized while arranging my notes that this moment held meanings that would direct my life. Two hundred eyes in that room, and another pair three time zones away, were watching to see if I had the stuff of a lawyer. Somewhere in the lecture hall the professor was asking me something, but I was too concerned with why my legs felt numb and my tongue so dry to hear him.

"I'll ask again, Mr. Toner," he said, his tone rising. "What were the precedents for *Yellow Cab v The State of New York?*"

I glanced up from my notes—that's a nice tie you're wearing, I thought—but I said nothing. A minute passed and still I said nothing.

"I'll even give you a hint, Mr. Toner. 'Yellow' is a color and 'New York' is a state. And a 'cab' is a vehicle you will soon be driving to make a living if you don't answer me soon."

There was laughter throughout the lecture hall, brief and nervous laughter, and then silence. Vast, aching silence. The silence of deserts, the silence of tombs. I wildly flipped notepages around with fingers that felt thick and stiff and heavy as yams. I mutilated page after page. And the silence stretched on. Amid the stillness of those agonizing minutes, however, I was able to think with laser clarity of other vital matters: of Tupperware lids and hash brown potatoes, of lip gloss and toenails, of crucifixes and bowling alleys. Why, I thought, must bowling balls be so heavy? What chance have old ladies and little kids with such a heavy thing?

Meanwhile, a law professor somewhere far outside of me was either helping or ridiculing me. I couldn't tell. All I knew was that in time I sat down in a ruined heap, feeling dark and shriveled, feeling like a tiny little raisin of a man.

I picked up my pen. In the margins of my notes, of my typed and arrowed and, in the end, entirely useless notes, I began to doodle.

With my eyes an inch from the page I doodled a circle, no bigger than a dime, that I darkened completely and then more deeply, my pen pressing down so firmly that I broke through one sheet of neat and typed notes down into another, and then another. I could feel outside my darkness the stare of an older man, a father, blinking like a leopard in a darker night. I lowered my moist eyes to the burrowing doodle.

And to me the doodle spoke: of a brain without a father's recall and agility, of a brain best left to teaching prepositions to children, of a brain that was, alas, a little bit boring.

The next day I withdrew from law school.

I thought about this while waiting with Cindy at the Sri Lanka airport for my father's arrival. The flight had been delayed twelve hours without any explanation, a delay that hadn't fazed us Lords of Idleness. But now it had landed, and in a few minutes my dad would step through that customs door and be the responsibility of this teacher and rather dull boy—not this lawyer, not this priest—for the next seven hundred hours. I turned that figure over in my head: *seven hundred* consecutive uninterrupted hours. That is a lot of time. I worried that if the snakes and heat and intestinal worms didn't get to him, then simple boredom with me might do him in.

Alongside the airport customs door stood the all-too-common sight of four soldiers with rifles. Two of them smoked Marlboros, one inspected his gun, another leered at Cindy. All four had that defiant look that comes from being at war so long that now they abided by their rules only. Next to me stood an Indian Sikh, turbaned and bearded, who belched up curry fumes every few minutes. Nearby, six Sri Lankan women in saris squatted in a circle, their limbs angled up high like grasshoppers. A cleaning woman approached us, pausing to reload her mouth with another betel leaf wrapped around a betel nut. She swept around us in wide arcs with a broom of tightly bound twigs, her barefoot toes splayed wide and flat from a lifetime without shoes.

*You have a lot to sweep, don't you?* Cindy said to her in Sinhala.

The woman stopped her twigs in midsweep, the Sikh stopped belching, the leering soldier stopped stroking his rifle—all frozen by the miraculous sound of Sinhala from a white woman's mouth. Before long Cindy was chatting with the woman in complex, perfect Sinhala, all spoken at a clip that left me in the dust. Cindy was the language legend of the Peace Corps, an accomplishment that drew crowds around her while I sat mute in a corner, feeling like a fool. Maybe my Sinhala never rose above the passable level because I was too busy practicing how to smile dumbly. I practiced it well, and here in the airport the cleaning woman, her lips rimmed with the deep scarlet of betel, saw that dumb smile and quickly hurried off, bent low like a reaper.

People from my father's flight began entering the waiting room. Out walked a Muslim woman shrouded in black cloth. Out walked five jittery tourists, probably Germans, clustered together in a tight molecule to avoid Third World diseases. Out walked an older Sri Lankan man in a sarong with wild shoots of hair flaring out of his ears, followed by a younger man who sniffed his mother's cheek in the Sri Lankan form of a kiss. Cindy noticed that this passenger, and then all the other passengers, had sand on their shoes. The six grasshopper women rose to greet their sister, who was pushing a cart stacked high with a TV, a VCR, a blender, and a dozen other electrical appliances. She had probably been a maid in the Middle East and was now, after two years, returning to her village home without electricity to display these appliances like icons. There was sand on her shoes.

More faces, more faces, but still no father. The Sikh to my right belched again, his curry fumes rising straight into my nose.

I imagined grabbing the loose end of his turban and quickly unraveling it, spinning him in a tight spiral like a skater at the end of a performance, centrifuging all the curry atoms out of his pores.

And then, impossible as it all was, there stood my father—my *father*, for Christ's sake, his gray hair wildly tufted like a troll doll's. In that moment before our eyes locked I felt a mixture of dread and panic. Here shuffling toward me was a very old and very disoriented man—his walk unsteady, his shoelaces untied, his wing tips all sandy.

At the sudden sight of us, though, he came alive. "Holy God, Jimmy and Cindy!" he exclaimed, spreading his arms wide like a vaudeville singer. "What a trip from hell!"

My first thought: I'm glad he remembers Cindy's name. For my father this was rare. A cross-wiring in his brain twisted his daughters-in-law's names, so that "Lainie" became "Lonnie" and "Katie" became "Kittie." But "Cindy" he got right, maybe because only she had the audacity to call him "John." While the others called him "Father" or nothing at all, Cindy thrust out her "John" with defiance. My dad liked that in her. "That's quite a modern gal you've got there, Jimmy," he'd say.

Here in the airport the modern gal ran to embrace my dad. I stood to the side, aware that at this moment when profound thoughts ought to be filling a son's soul—my *father!* the creator of my eyes, my skin!—all I could really think was that this man was wearing a lot of clothes. Undershirt, flannel shirt, tweed jacket. His pants were wool. His socks were black. His shoes, mottled with mystery flecks of sand, were probably the first wing tips to ever step on Sri Lankan soil. Yukon fashions in ninety-six-degree heat and ninety percent humidity, even at 8 A.M.

My dad's face widened into a broad grin at the touch of Cindy. As their hug lingered I noticed trickles of sweat running down the channels of his neck. This is not normal, I thought, nor are the strange white spots on his skin. This man is hot. This is a man who might wilt unto death right here, right now. After all, he *is* seventy-four years old, and though this hardy Irishman has only the one problem of a weak bladder to empty often in the night, the fact remains that he *is* seventy-four. His ventricles and kneecaps and pancreas have all been working nonstop since World War I. What would I do if my father, right on this airport floor, suddenly clutched his heart and gasped, "Help, oh Jimmy, oh God," and fell to my feet? What did I know about CPR? Could I call on the Sikh to give my dad mouth-to-mouth with curry belches?

Worried, I fanned his neck and took off his tweed jacket. He didn't seem to notice, even when the sleeve of the jacket snagged on the rosary beads encircling his wrist. He just kept hugging Cindy, which I thought was getting a bit excessive. After all, *I* was the son here. *I'm* the one responsible for all of this. Then I saw that Cindy was crying, an emotion so beyond my simple relief that my dad hadn't keeled over and died that I thought: The ways of women are beyond reckoning. Cry. Go ahead and cry and hug while I just stand here like a butler holding his jacket.

My dad's odor rose off that jacket like dragon's breath, hot and rancid and faintly grassy. It was a familiar odor that brought to mind those times twenty-five years earlier when I wore my dad's shirts to grade school. I would heist them from his closet each morning, then strut into my eighth-grade class, confident that my pink pinstriped shirt with cufflinks could override my bland looks and impress the class goddess, Sheila Hart. Of course she ignored me, but I wondered in the Sri Lanka airport if it was this peculiar dragon odor, and not my gargoyle face, that repulsed her.

Finally, my dad stopped hugging Cindy and turned to me. "Jimmy, Jimmy, Jimmy."

Before I knew what to do, before I knew if I should shake his hand or embrace him or hoist him onto my shoulders, I pressed my palms together beneath my chin and said, "Ayubowan, Dad."

He took a half-step back.

Cindy smoothed down his wild hair and explained that *ayubowan* is the Sri Lankan welcome. "It means that the god in me is greeting the god in you. Try it."

"No, no, no. Language lessons later, kids. For now I'm just damn glad to get my feet on the ground." He looked down. "Will you look at these shoes, Cindy. Shot to hell, that's what they are. Sand. Never seen so much of it in all your life."

With my *ayubowan* left hanging in the air, without so much as a handshake between us, my dad began to recount the story of his eventful flight to Sri Lanka. "Oh, kids, don't get me started. And whatever you do, don't whisper a word of this to Mother." He told us about a bomb threat on his flight that forced the Air Lanka jet to emergency-land at an airport in Saudi Arabia. "So there I was, your old man, sliding down the chute and running out into the desert—part scared, part thrilled. The *Sahara*, kids! Never thought I'd live to see the Sahara. So there I go running . . . oh, maybe you can't call what I do 'running,' but anyhow there I go loping and limping out into who-the-hell-knows-where. Sure, I'm worried this thing might blow up but, holy God, kids, this was the *Sahara*! Dunes, camels—I saw it all! So there I am out there in the middle of the Sahara—jeez, I love just saying the word—and all of a sudden I start to sink. Wet sand starts oozing up and up and over my brand new wing tips. Oh, mother's gonna kill me. A hundred bucks, brand new, and now look at 'em: Shot to hell."

There's nothing like a good story to invigorate an Irishman. By the time he had finished, my father was sparkling and animated. As much as I felt responsible for having put him through such an ordeal, I was delighted at the story it had given him, a story that would get repeated a hundred times back in Cleveland, each time with more exaggeration until my dad would tell his audience that he leaped on a camel that galloped away fast as a thoroughbred.

"Just promise me one thing, kids," he whispered, drawing us close like conspirators. "Not a word of this to mother or we're goners for sure. And not a word to Malone. I don't want him telling me I got what I deserved for flying a jungle airline just to save a buck or two."

We led my dad to the foreign-exchange counter. He interlocked his arm into Cindy's when the cleaning woman bumped into him and the Sikh belched behind him, and when he saw two soldiers pressing their rifles into the neck of a kneeling man, my father tightened his grip and looked away. At the exchange counter a teller behind a thick slab of glass counted money at flickering speed. My dad withdrew his wallet, its leather shiny and rounded, and thumbed through so much money that it astonished me. Cindy and I earned about two dollars a day, so seeing all this money in one spot reminded me of the different world my father inhabited. At the sight of all that money a math problem entered my head: If a retired Cleveland judge with two thousand dollars exchanged his money for forty Sri Lankan rupees to the dollar, and if he only spent thirty rupees per day, how long could this white man live in this country? And would his wife miss his tomato soup? And would he still wear wool pants?

My father leaned into the speaker and asked the teller, "Do you good folks take good American money?" The teller kept counting, and when I explained to my dad that these people didn't speak English, he rapped on the window and waved his arms, shouting, "MONEY! ME GIVE! YOU GIVE! AMERICA! MONEY GOOD!"

I translated this Tarzan talk into Sinhala for the teller. He looked up at my father and, wobbling his head from side to side, said, "Hah-hah-hah-hah-hah-hah-hah."

My dad turned to me, his tight jaw holding the resentment at having the almighty American dollar rejected. "Now that's a shocker," he said. "A bank that doesn't want good fresh money."

"Give the guy your money, Dad," I said.

He looked at me as if I were a child that caught on to things very slowly. "But he doesn't take it, Jimmy. Didn't you just see him shake his head and laugh at me?"

"He shook his head 'yes,' and that wasn't a laugh."

"Not a laugh? I know a laugh and I know a 'no.' Cindy, you saw it, didn't you?"

She explained to him that the Sri Lankan "yes" shake is the American "no" shake, and that their "hah-hah-hah-hah-hah-hah" is like our "right right right." "That's your first cultural lesson here, John," she said. "Welcome to the other side of the planet."

My dad looked from Cindy to the teller and then back to me, unsure if he was the butt of some practical joke. That there was no joke deflated him. If the bedrock symbols for "yes" and "no" are arbitrary, then what? Just how alien *is* this place?

This encounter with the unique ways of another culture was, I knew, just a prologue for him. There would be the customers in restaurants spitting food on the floor, the men holding men's hands, the "go away" waves actually meaning "come here." There would be the Buddhist temples and the rubble of war, the honoring of animals and the use of the left hand in ways unimagined in Cleveland. And I wondered if an old white man who comes to Sri Lanka wearing a flannel shirt could be ready for any of this.

He slid the thick wad of bills beneath the bank window. The teller exchanged the monochromatic American money for a Sri Lankan packet shimmering and exotic as tropical birds. My dad put half the money into his wallet. It barely closed, and when he squeezed it into his back pocket it bulged like a tumor. Then, glancing quickly around, he unbuttoned his shirt and unzipped a money belt girding his stomach. "A gift from Malone," my dad said. "He tells me this joint is crawling with thieves that'll steal the lungs right out of your chest if you don't watch out." He stuffed the pouch with money, then again scanned for robbers before tucking everything back into place.

"Hey, Dad," I said, "that's a pretty nifty secret you've got there."

He wobbled his head sideways as the teller had done, saying, "Hah-hah-hah-hah-hah-hah-hah-hah."

At that moment I just couldn't help it: I loved the guy. This semi-stranger is my father, this one with the Yukon clothes and the sandy wing tips, the one who feels so wily about his secret kangaroo pouch. He has come to visit me from across the planet, all alone, his old white rump punctured with shots of hepatitis and typhoid and rabies, and he probably wonders as much as I do how this whole thing will come off.

I wanted to touch him.

So I reached across the expanse of thirty-four years to wipe away the sweat gathering against the collar of his flannel shirt. My fingers against his neck. My flesh against his flesh.

He flinched at the touch.

2

My father sat in the front seat of the taxi on the drive into Colombo, the capital. In the early morning the temperature was already well over ninety degrees, typical for April, the hottest and most humid month of the year. From the back seat I could see the colors of my father's flannel collar darkening with sweat. Before reaching the hotel his entire shirt would be saturated, his entire face damp. Though I felt an impulse to pat him dry, I just sat far back in my seat and watched the scenery.

We drove on the left side of the road, dodging bicyclists and schoolchildren and bulls, and when we barely missed a head-on with a truck overloaded with coconut husks, I started to notice my dad's shudders and winces. He tried to murmur prayers and finger his rosary beads, but more often he would cover his eyes and whimper, "Oh my God, oh my blessed God!" I advised him to look anywhere but at the road. Cindy distracted him by pointing out the parrots flying over the paddy fields, and the water buffaloes pulling the plows, and the unusual scarecrows on the farms. "See those dark things sticking out of the ground," she said, "the ones that curl up? They're coconut branches the farmers use as scarecrows because they look like cobras. You see? They're rearing up and . . . Are you even looking out there?"

"Lanes! Does anyone follow lanes in this country! Or am I just an old codger who respects the law? Holy God,"—he grabbed the driver's arm—"watch out!"

A bus swerved back into its lane at the last instant and our driver, nonchalantly dangling his wrist over the steering wheel, laughed, then violently sped up into the center of oncoming traffic with his bright lights flashing.

"Dad, look over to the right. There's an elephant carrying a log, and over there at the temple, a monkey. Imagine, Dad: a monkey!" When he finally did look away from the road, he asked about the police gathered around the column of burning tires. I told him it was nothing and instead pointed out the man in a loincloth shinnying up a coconut palm. "He's gathering a sap that'll turn into alcohol. When he finishes with that tree he just tightrope walks over to the next and the next. See all those ropes up there? Maybe you'd like to walk them."

He rolled up his sleeves. "My God it's hot. Sweltering. Malone told me this heat was no worse than Florida but believe you me this is no Florida. Never felt a heat like this in all my life. How can you kids stand it?"

Soon the sights of rice farms and coconut plantations gave way to the rubble of Colombo. Traffic, as always, was heavy, our taxi sharing the deeply rutted road with bicycles and trucks, cows, mango carts, buses spewing thick diesel exhaust into our cab. My dad covered his mouth with a monogrammed JJT handkerchief. From each of the vehicles around us came a distinct horn or bell: the air blast of trucks, the timid penguin squawk from the three-wheeled taxis called *trishaws*. None of these horns served any purpose because all were in use at once.

Our taxi stopped behind a long line at a traffic light, one of only eight in the entire country. Two cars passed through every five minutes when it turned green. We inched, and we waited, our driver never once lifting his hand off the horn. The sweat on my dad's neck was beaded and flowing. I told him about gas prices and bus fares, flooding problems and garbage systems—anything to get his mind off the noise, the dirt, the heat. But none of it triggered any response from him, just a quicker clatter of his rosary beads.

Green light, move an inch; red light, stop and bake. I looked up, and there looming over our heads were two colossal movie posters, one an enraged Rambo and the other a seductive V. J. Kumaratunga, the country's film idol, who a year earlier had been assassinated at a political rally. They were cool and suave up there, removed from our traffic jams and our horns, above the heat that rose off the asphalt and through the thin floorboards of our taxi, cooking my feet. I slung my arm outside the window but the hot metal of the door singed my skin.

My dad swiveled around to us, his face now an alarming red. "Pretty soon, kids, I'll be needing a little water."

Cindy patted his shoulder. "We'll get you something right away."

A man selling Fantas weaved his way among the unmoving cars. Cindy bought four and handed one to my dad. He brought the bottle to his lips and then stopped, examining the rim and its chipped edge. He muttered something about Malone and germs and then passed the bottle to the driver, who swallowed it in one swift gulp while still laying on his horn.

A woman balancing two fifty-pound sacks of rice on her head sidled through the cars, as did a child carrying a tray of gum and pencils. Another man carrying a placard of lottery tickets screamed into our window. Meanwhile, a soldier leaning against the hood of our taxi smoked an entire cigarette without our cab moving an inch. He flicked the butt into a beggar's face and then sauntered away, punching the sides of cars for no apparent reason.

Our taxi moved ahead a few yards; five minutes later we moved ahead a few more. A beggar woman with one infant on a nipple and a naked boy on her hip spotted us, the Great White Tourist.

20

While moving toward my father, her face sagged into an expression of great misery and hunger. She held her palm out limply a few inches from my dad's face, and with the other hand she scraped away the yellow crust beneath her baby's nose. At the sight of my father the baby screeched. All of this bewildered my dad, whose only experiences with beggars in Cleveland had been phone salesmen and, I suppose, his seven children. He turned around and asked us what to do.

"Give her a few rupees," Cindy said, handing him some coins, then turned to the woman and explained in sophisticated Sinhala who we were. They spoke fast and full of idioms that I understood for three seconds before settling into a corner with my familiar dumb smile. When my dad asked for a translation, I invented some likely dialogue until Cindy, her face screwed up in contempt, turned away from the beggar and said, "That's not even close."

It didn't matter. My dad, his face screwed up into a different shade of contempt, was preoccupied with the palm of the beggar boy wagging too close to his nose. Careful not to touch the skin, my dad dropped a coin that bounced off the boy's palm and rolled beneath the truck alongside us. The truck driver watched the boy crawl beneath his truck and, with a crooked grin, blared his horn, shuddering our cab and sending the baby into new shrieks and spasms. We moved up half an inch. Suddenly the baby grabbed my dad's finger and stuck it in his mouth. The other child, coin in hand, tried to snatch my dad's rosary until the cabby, enraged, smacked the boy's hand. *Go, you rats!* he shouted, balling his hand into a fist. *Go this second or I'll run you over with my car. Now go!*

While they trotted away to another car my father stared in shock at the baby spit dripping down his finger. I wondered if he was considering lopping the whole finger off. Instead he just wiped it frantically with his JJT handkerchief, wiping it over and over as if sanding away the skin. Then he tightened his grip on his rosary and looked down at his feet, and continued to look down even when I pointed out a monkey swinging from tree to tree in front of the president's palace.

⚘

Eventually we arrived at the hotel. For the first night my father insisted that we stay in the country's finest hotel, the Colombo Lake House; I agreed, knowing that from then on he'd be subjected to the more primitive conditions in Sri Lanka's interior. Because of the war, the Lake House had lowered its rates from $110 per night to $20 to attract tourists, yet still only a fraction of its rooms were occupied. This meant that hotel workers like the doorman, who was asleep when we pulled into the broad apron of the Lake House, had to struggle to survive as long as the war persisted.

The cab driver tooted his horn, startling the doorman awake. Jumping to his feet, he adjusted his fez and realigned the gold buttons on his white tunic before stepping to my father's side of the car. He examined his reflection in the window and then, opening the door, bowed deeply in a flourish of ceremony.

"To the enchanted isle of Serendib," he proclaimed in English, "I greet you with all due humbleness."

For the doorman, my dad's arrival was indeed serendipitous, a word originating from an early name for Sri Lanka, "Serendib." European sailors who landed here accidentally, discovering all the spices and gems and tropical fruit of Serendib, later applied the island's name to anything valuable found by chance. For the doorman, we were valuable because we were white. White equals money, so the doorman was quick to extend his arm to my father.

"My good sir," the doorman said, remaining in his bow, "please accept without hesitation my humble succor."

My father leaned heavily on the doorman's arm and rose unsteadily from the car. Once on his feet my dad swayed, his face mottled pink and white. He wiped the patina of city grime off his forehead with his handkerchief, then looked at the swath of black grit covering the JJT monogram.

"Holy God," he grumbled.

The doorman's forehead wrinkled. "Is the sir feeling adequate? Shall I in humbleness procure the services of our establishment's doctor? A fine doctor he is at that, I might with liberty add, sir."

My father's eyes squinted into the sun. "I'm okay. Just could use a little water is all. Clean water. Water in a bottle."

The doorman bowed and hurried away, pausing briefly to shoo away a legless beggar on a skateboard raising up to us a split, jagged Coke can rattling with coins. While the doorman was gone, my dad asked about his peculiar English. Cindy explained that before 1948 Sri Lanka was an English colony, the last of many European countries that had occupied this island. Under the British, the Sri Lankans learned and spoke a formal Oxford English, especially servants like the doorman who, attempting to impress the great white sahib, would elevate their vocabulary with odd archaisms. When Sri Lanka gained its independence in 1948, there went most traces of English, except for fossils like the doorman whose English, they felt, gave them status and dignity.

The doorman returned. He held a bottle of water up high with both hands, his fez tilted and nearly falling. "To the good sir I bring the elixir of life itself. Do with pleasure imbibe and feel spring flowers in the belly of sir."

While my father drank, Cindy and I entered the lobby wide eyed. We had almost forgotten what this opulence was like: chandeliers, thick carpets, fountains with inlaid tiles, air conditioning. *Air conditioning!* All of it astonished us in contrast to our village home in Bandarawela made of mud and stones and cow dung. My feelings about these comforts were ambivalent. On the one hand I realized that the cost of one of these eight crystal chandeliers could equip the villagers of Bandarawela with books and medicine for a decade; on the other hand, this air conditioning felt damn good.

Meanwhile, over at the registration counter there was something desperately wrong with my father. He was frantic, slapping and squeezing each pocket again and again. He called over to me. "It's my wallet, Jimmy! It's my wallet and my rosary and oh, good God, they're gone! Stolen, gone!"

This was no mere wallet, I knew. It was the *bank*, swollen with a thousand fortunes to release any of these Sri Lankans—the sweeper woman, the beggar family, the Fez—from their treadmill lives.

"It was that lady!" my dad snarled. "That dirty filthy one with the baby. I know it. I know that kid was just part of the act. Malone, he warned me all about it: one distracts while the other goes for the goods. It's a racket!"

No sooner did that thought get developed when the cab driver ran in, his bare feet slapping on the marble. "Mama hoyagatta!" he shouted. "Mama oyaage pombekupetay hoyagatta!"

He held the wallet above his head, the rosary beads entwined around his fingers. I thought: Run, cabby! Run away with that fortune in your hands! End your cabby suffering of soot and blare, of sitting at stoplights in your fiery metal can. Run and sip piña coladas in a turquoise pool and go join Rambo and V. J. up on the billboard. Run, and run away with a clear conscience: The old guy still has a stomach-pouch crammed with rupees.

The driver handed the wallet and rosary over to my father. "Holy God, kids, will you take a look here!" my dad said, thumbing through the ream in his wallet. "It's all here, every last rupert! Oh, my good man, thank you, thank you, a thousand times thank you!" He shook the cabby's hand too vigorously, then remembering that English didn't work here, he shouted, "THANK YOU! ME HAPPY! YOU GOOD! HAPPY HAPPY!"

My dad's Tarzan English was starting to bother me. He asked us if he should give the driver some kind of reward, and when I suggested the rosary, he buried it in his pocket. "It's a nice thought but . . . well, you know, it's a sentimental thing. From my mother, she brought it with her from Ireland and, well heck, what's a rosary to these non-Catholics, anyway? It's money these folks are after, so what's a ballpark figure, Jimmy? A fifty? A hundred?"

The doorman stuck his head between my father and me. "Pardon me with the duest of all respects," he said, tipping his fez, "but without my succor our benevolent driver fails to locate the sir. He drives off, as you Americans say, into the sunset. Of course, to help the sir on his inaugural day in Serendib gives to humble me a satisfaction of exceeding gratification."

I pulled my dad aside by the elbow, whispering, "Give the driver a hundred or two. That's only four or five bucks American. And as for this other clown"—I had an impulse to tell my dad to tip the doorman with a thesaurus—"just ignore him for now. We'll tip him when we leave."

My father spread wide the lips of his wallet and, licking his fingers, separated a couple of bills from the brick. The Fez caught sight of the vault and whistled.

"It is in memory most recent," he said, "that I, your most humble servant, recall with delicious reverie the gift of water to a parched sir. On the wind I ponder the life I save with joy unbound. Joy is my daily bread, but let us not forget our thirst."

My dad shook two hundred rupees into the driver's hand. "Here you go, my good man. Can't thank you enough. Hah-hah-hah-hah-hah and all that. Now you go buy yourself some new shoes or a new horn or whatever. SHOES! HORN! You know—BEEP! BEEP!"

We were heading for the elevator when the Fez stepped in front of us. "Sir, and son of sir, and gracious delicate daughter of sir. It was with copious goodwill that I directed this driver to you, this common laborer devoid of foot apparel and not a word of the King's English in his peasant head. Without my gracious service, heartbreak would abound."

Cindy stepped around him to press the elevator button.

"In our fair land of Serendib," he persisted, "graciousness begets graciousness."

We boarded the elevator.

"Sir, allow me to be direct. A reward to the barefoot lackey should be commensurate with—" But the door had closed on his plea, his face at the last moment looking very old and very sad.

My father had no pity for the Fez on the elevator ride up. His spirit was celebrating the miracle of the returned wallet and rosary, an event of epic meaning to him.

"Not a rupert gone," he said, shaking his head in disbelief. "Here's this black fellow I don't know from Adam, no doubt dirt poor, probably's got ten, fifteen kids all without shoes all living in . . . in what? A hut or a shack or just cardboard. And he gives it *all* back. Every last tempting rupert to a guy—"

"It's 'rupee,' Dad," I said. "Not 'rupert.'"

"Well, whatever you want to call it, I call it a miracle. And I call it a sign that God is shining on us today."

In fact my dad had always measured his standing with God by some event having to do with money. Today God was shining upon him, but usually my dad ended up on the short end. Once as a child I remember seeing my father at a Nebraska gas station, standing defeated before a Coke machine. It had just eaten his quarter. I watched him from the back seat of our Delta 88, trembling at the sight of my dad bashing the machine, each fist a blow at faith and the capitalist system and the sport God was making of his life.

"Oh for heaven's sake, John," my mom pleaded, pushing her butterfly sunglasses up her nose, "just use another quarter and let's be on the road."

"It's not the quarter, Lil. You know and I know and those low-down crooks at Coke know that—"

"The principle, the principle," my mom nodded. "Of course it's a matter of principle. But for now, John, would you *please* just drop in another quarter so we can get on the road. Here, take mine."

He paused and looked around. "This is not right, Lil, and this will not stand."

I slunk lower and lower until I was at eye level with the back seat of the Delta 88. I could see the raised floral print of the upholstery filled with bread crumbs—*my* bread crumbs. I generally sat on my white-bread and grape-jelly sandwiches, imprinting them with the floral stamp of the seat before eating them. An artist was at work in the back of the Delta 88. After a little while the artist rose up to window level and saw that the Coke machine had swallowed yet another of my father's quarters.

"Oh God!" my tormented father howled to the wind. "Oh merciless God to whom I have worshipped in church *every* damn morning at 6:30 A.M. and to whom I have said two daily rosaries for *forty years*. WHY DOST THOU TOY"—and here his fists punched the sky, a broken man, a King Lear at a Texaco station—"WITH MY *MONEY!*"

Thirty years later in the Lake House elevator all justice had been restored. "Let me tell you kids something," my dad said. "God is at work in this country, in that cab driver. Not one single rupert . . . er, ru*peeeee*"—he bared his teeth at me—"is missing, and so that man walks away a very rich man indeed."

A Korean couple boarded the elevator. When the doors closed, I noticed the woman examining her face in the reflection, her eyes and cheeks swollen and blue. Suddenly, panting quick and loud, she turned to her partner and slugged him hard across the face, shrieking a high-pitched banshee wail. She kicked the man over and over until, on floor six, the doors opened and she tossed him out like a rogue from a Western saloon. My father backed into a corner.

The doors closed and the four of us rode up, silent and tense. We looked up at the floor numbers, then down and then up, then

27

over at the operating license (last checked six years ago), then down to our fingernails.

My father cleared his throat. "Nope, not a rupert taken. Not a one. I can only wonder what would've happened with that wallet in Cleveland. You know, with a Cleveland cabby, most of those folks don't think of the law straight away."

The woman's shoulders shook, and I could see in the gold reflection of the door that tears were dripping through her cupped hands covering her face.

"Nope, nope, nope," my dad said. "Not a single rupert taken."

Inside our hotel room the Third World was sealed out. At first the luxuries thrilled me. For the two previous years Cindy and I had slept on wooden slats covered by a wafer-thin mat, so at the sight of this thick mattress I jumped onto it like a trampoline, bouncing up and down, vaulting from one king-sized bed over to the other. It was fun, and when Cindy told me to behave and sit down, I bounced even higher just to irritate her.

After a while I explored the miracles of the bathroom: a phone, a hair dryer, toilet paper (first sheet folded!), hot water from a tap. I stepped into the bathtub and luxuriated in my first hot shower in over a year. Each scorching droplet so massaged me, so soothed me, that I imagined this water pipe going up through the Lake House roof and up through the clouds and up to an all-beneficent Shower God, grinning in a fatherly way at dirty Jimmy Toner. When I began to suffocate from all the steam, I stepped out, dried off, and flushed the toilet: blue dye! I flushed it again with Cindy alongside me, trying to persuade her of the beauty, the spirit, indeed, the *poetry* of the flush toilet. She was searching for an adjective for me—"overdramatic," "silly"—when my dad knocked on the door.

"'Scuse me, coming on through. Hope I'm not interrupting anything romantic, but I need to use the . . . jeez, it's steamy in here. I need to use the sink on these wing tips. Just look at 'em. What a shame." He blasted water into the little wing-tip holes, then removed the hair dryer from its holster on the wall and aimed it at the shoes. "Mother's gonna kill me," he shouted above the dryer's whine. "Two weeks old and they're shot to hell."

I was busy in the next room bouncing on the beds, pretending I was a circus acrobat falling from a great height to my death. I asked Cindy to play along with me, to be the grieving widow holding her crushed Bulgarian husband in her arms, but she wasn't listening. She was standing at the window looking down on the traffic and out at the ocean, and she stayed expressionless even when I told her my theory of the Shower God. I turned my attention to an air-conditioning vent and pressed my face against it.

My dad walked out of the bathroom. "Who's the patron saint of lost causes?" he asked. He was wearing only black socks and underwear—white, sagging, old-man underwear. He held up both hands covered like hooves with the two disfigured wing tips. "Because what I've got here, kids, is a pair of lost causes. What I've got here is a waste of good money."

"What we've really got here," I said, "is you in need of some clothes. I brought a sarong that you might want to try on. It'll keep you cool, too."

"Oh no, Jimmy, there'll be none of that. Malone told me all about those things, those skirts. Your father isn't about to go native on anybody." He shook off one hoof in order to unzip his suitcase, then pulled out a bottle of Scotch. "This here will keep me plenty cool. Say, Jimmy, whadya say we order up a little ice, glasses, maybe some soda." Suddenly concern darkened his face. "Whoa, now: the ice. Malone, he had me promise him that I'd steer clear of all ice, especially hotel ice. 'Let that hotel ice touch your lips,' he says, 'and you'll be close friends with the toilet from then on out.'"

Cindy, not quite sure at what part of my dad's anatomy to look, said to the floor, "I think that in a place like this, John, the ice and the water are purified. Especially the ice. I wouldn't—"

"Oh no! They'll tell you it's okay and you'll think it's okay but Malone warned me it's not, that it's packed solid with bugs that'll knock you to your knees." He paused for a moment in thought, his left hoof nudging his chin. "Oh, the hell with that jackass Malone. Order us up a bucket of ice, Jimmy."

Ten minutes later the man from room service knocked on the door. My father, the one-hoofed goat in diapers, opened the door and stood there with no more shame than a swimmer in a Speedo. The young Sri Lankan man stepped back at the sight of my dad, then quickly handed over the ice and a newspaper. Confused about where to look, he said to the ceiling, "To you a paper, gift of my country, I welcome to lovely island yes." He swiveled and abruptly left, probably holding that impression of Americans as perverts forever in his mind.

My dad handed me the newspaper, and I could tell by its thinness that the editors must be in trouble. The Sri Lankan government boasted that this democratic nation embraced free speech, yet this was neither a democracy (soldiers stuffed the ballot box) nor a land of free speech. Speech was controlled indirectly. The government allotted newsprint to the papers according to how flattering, or how critical, the editors portrayed President Premadasa. A critical piece one day meant a meager paper the next; an ingratiating piece one day meant a thick paper the next. Most editors, catching on quickly to the rules of this game, turned their front pages into Premadasa propaganda: Premadasa touching the lepers, Premadasa blessed by Buddha, Premadasa loved by the schoolchildren.

While I glanced at the headlines, my father was hard at work. "Now tell me again what you kids fancy. Scotch? A nip of

Tanqueray?" He measured his own drink in a shot glass with the care and precision of a chemist. "You kids just name your poison."

Cindy declined but I accepted, partly for the novelty of tasting alcohol before noon, partly because there was bonding potential here. With Scotch in hand there was no telling how much the souls of my father and me might interweave.

"I assume that'll be with ice, Jimmy," he said, dipping the tongs into the ice bucket.

I slapped his back. "But of course, Dad. Load it right on up."

"Then here ya be," he said, raising his glass, "and to hell with Malone."

"To hell with Malone!"

And there we stood, he in his underwear, me in my thin cotton pants, sipping our Scotches on ice with great maturity. As the alcohol began to work on my brain, I thought: Damn if this isn't *bonding!*

"Now, Jimmy, not a word of that bomb to your mother."

"It's dead and buried as far as I'm concerned. Kapoot."

He began to chuckle. "Oh, but Jimmy, can you imagine her face if I told her. A bomb! Oh, Lordy, I think her false teeth would fly right out of her mouth."

I nearly spat out an ice cube. "Her mouth, it'd be puckered like a drawstring," I said, which I thought such a clever image that I repeated it.

"Oh, it's a blessed thing she never came over here with me, Jimmy. Can you imagine her coming down that chute and then running out into the desert?"

"She'd never jump, Dad. Never."

"You're right on that one. She'd claw out the stewardess's eyes before she'd take that first step. Now, Jimmy, how's about I warm up your drink a tad?"

"You got any more Scotch, Pops?" (Pops? Had I just called him "Pops"?)

31

"Not enough Scotch to wash an elephant, if that's what you're asking."

Lord Almighty, this bonding was grand! And *important*. So when Cindy turned away from the window and said, "Maybe we ought to get going so your father can rest," I was sure that this experience was beyond a woman's reckoning.

"We'll go when we go, and when we go we'll go," I said, and regretted immediately that something so idiotic had flown out of my mouth. Cindy turned back to the window. "Dad, if Malone knew we were sucking on hotel ice cubes he'd be——"

"That Malone is a good fella, Jimmy. A good family man." He sipped his drink. "I just wish he'd remove that burr from his ass every so often."

We shot our heads back and laughed mightily. Cindy stood up abruptly. "Let's go," she said. "Or if you're not then I am and I'll just meet you later."

My dad put down his drink. "Whoa, I nearly forgot! The goodies!" He hoisted his suitcase onto the bed and opened it wide, letting fall onto the bed the gifts we'd be giving to Sri Lankans when we left in six months. Some of the gifts we had specifically requested—jump ropes, books, crayons, glue, T-shirts—while others, like a jigsaw puzzle of Houston and a poster of Newark, were either my mom's humor or her lunacy at work.

"You drove your mother ragged getting this stuff," my dad said, replenishing his Scotch. "K-Mart, Woolworth's, Wal-Mart—you name it, she went to it. Every day she'd come home with more junk. And that Twist it thing . . . yellow? lime?"

"Lemon," Cindy said. "Lemon Twist. You got it?"

He spat out some of his drink like a bad slapstick act. "Lemon Twist! We searched high and low for that thing and when we finally found it, holy good God it has"—his eyes widened at the modern world—"a *computer* inside it! Imagine that, a little bitty computer to count the revolutions. And believe you me it's no three bucks like you said, Jimmy. Nothing is, nothing at all, so get ready for a shocker when you come on home. What the hell is it, anyway, this twist thing?" Cindy explained that it was simply a kid's jumping game in which a rope connected at the center to a lemon-like ball revolved in a circle at different speeds. My dad nodded. "Sounds like something I'd like to give a try."

My attention was elsewhere. "Cookies!" I shouted, shredding open a package. More than just sugar and chocolate, this package was home. It was mother, her kitchen redolent of sweet batter, wiping her hands on her apron before opening up the oven. "My mom sent me cookies!"

My dad chuckled. "Let me tell you, Lil just went crazy over you kids. Say, Jimmy, before you dig in there, can I offer you a warm-up?"

"Yeah, just a sec. Eight, nine . . ." I counted up the cookies. "There's fifteen here, Cindy. That means we each get five."

My dad raised a hoof. "Only one for me, Jimmy. Doesn't sit well with the bowels."

"Good," I said. "That means seven apiece, Cindy."

"Little territorial, aren't we?"

"I'm just trying to be fair here, that's all."

"Fair? Petty, if you ask me."

I ignored her. I held out my glass to my dad, purposely letting the back of my wrist rub against his arm to feel the warm camaraderie conducting between us. It was happening, father-son bonding, and it (or was it the alcohol?) gave me the shivers.

"Hey, kids," my dad said, turning his suitcase upside down, "there's lots more goodies." Out tumbled a box of Bisquick, three rolls of toilet paper, a white Totes umbrella, two spray cans of mosquito repellent, a week's worth of Cleveland sports pages. I picked up the last two items, a green Gatorade water bottle and a Cleveland Indians baseball cap.

"Hey hey hey," my dad protested, grabbing both out of my hands. "The hat is mine and the bottle's my lifeline. Malone gave it to me.

Told me not to go anywhere without my own water, though where I'm supposed to get pure water around this joint is still a mystery."

His tone jarred me, and suddenly the whole scene jarred me. Pure water and air conditioning, flush toilets and hair dryers, cookies and Scotch. Quickly sobered, I saw this scene for what it was: three white Americans in an American world, sitting on a two-foot-thick mattress with crisp sheets. This is what my dad would want for the next seven hundred hours. We could watch CNN, order up scrambled eggs, gaze out our window during cocktail hour. After a month my dad could buy slides in the gift shop and, back in America, lie to his friends, "This slide of a jungle waterfall, that's when the kids and I rode elephants for three days, eating nothing but bamboo and grubs."

This is what he wants. For seven hundred hours he wants Scotch and TV and light talk so we can continue doing what we've done our whole lives: amuse ourselves to death. This trip to Sri Lanka, then, could be as jolly as a day at Disneyland, a day full of processed food and swept sidewalks and safe rides, all rewarding you in the end with that sick, bloated feeling that comes from too much amusement.

Enough. Enough of this antiseptic world, where truck horns and tropical heat and beggars with crusty noses are sealed out by these windows. Enough of me not knowing my dad and him not knowing me. I'm bored by it, and I'm bored by living life in the shadows. It's time, Dad, time for us to step out and meet a few demons waiting for us on our journey—a journey into either our darkness or our light.

So sleep well tonight, Dad. I'll give you thirty more hours of that mattress and those ice cubes, thirty more hours with your arms clinging to the edge of the pool before we risk it all and swim out together to the deep end. Out there is a world more primitive than you ever imagined, a world on the other side of the globe stripped clean of all your familiar words, gestures, and customs.

On the far edge of your life you gave me the gift of coming here to Sri Lanka. My return gift will be to rip you out of this room and to terrify you.

So drink well that final Scotch. On my way out of the room I'll take both bottles of alcohol and throw them away, later lying to you that the cleaning lady must have stolen them.

Until then, sleep well.

3

Cindy and I returned to the hotel the next morning to rouse my dad. When he didn't respond to my loud knocks, I began to fear that the Fez had broken in to steal his wallet, leaving my dad bound and gagged. Either that, or he now lay in a drunken heap on the bathroom floor, his spit pooled beneath a gaping mouth. I knocked harder with the heel of my palm.

Eventually the door opened a slit. "Huh . . . who there?" my dad said, squinting his eyes. His hair stood at jagged angles; his cheeks held deep creases of sleep like pirate scars. "You ice boy?"

"It's me, Dad. C'mon, let's get moving."

He looked confused, flipping through the Rolodex in his brain that cataloged all the voices of his life. When it matched up to mine, he moaned, knowing that this voice was attached to arms eager to drag him out of this air-conditioned American cocoon. He turned and zigzagged back to his bed, his body tacking against the headwinds of fatigue, hangover, and fear. With the hand that held his rosary beads, he pulled the covers over his head and wrapped himself up tight.

Cindy and I stood over him. "He looks like a giant burrito," I whispered to her.

"Let's let him sleep."

I shook him. "C'mon, Dad. Wake up or I'll pour tap water down your throat." The burrito rolled over, pulling the sheet tighter over his head. "What are you going to do, sleep this trip away?"

Cindy put her hand on my arm. "Maybe we should let him sleep a while longer. After all, the poor guy did cross twelve time zones."

"He's had enough sleep."

"Leave him alone. We'll come back tonight."

"WAKE UP, DAD!" I shouted. I hoisted him into a sitting position, the sheet still wrapped around his head. "Get dressed or we'll put you in a boxing ring with that Korean lady."

"Leave me be," he murmured weakly. "Have you no respect for your elders?"

Cindy tried pulling me away. "Let him down. Give him all the sleep he wants."

My dad's finger came through the sheet, pointing at me. "Listen well to that woman. She's a genius."

Of course I knew he needed more sleep, but I had my own needs, too: revenge. With each jostle of his body I remembered more and more clearly those winter mornings when my dad did the jostling. Every morning he would shake my brother Joe and me awake to go to Mass at 6:30 A.M. From our sweet warm beds he would lead us through the blue cold, two little boys bundled fat and alien as astronauts, flanking my father wearing only a topcoat. Our boots squeaked on the packed snow. Tusks of steam flared out of our nostrils. At the church door the rush of heat fogged up our glasses, causing us to bump into each other. Once inside the church I longed even more for sleep. Incense, a twisted man bleeding on a cross, doddering worshipers murmuring like the deranged—none of this was the stuff of my boyhood dreams.

But one cold morning some comedy descended upon Joe and me that startled us awake. At the most solemn part of the Mass, when the eyelids of two little boys were drooping lower and lower, old Father Weber raised his arms to God and trumpeted a loud, echoing, unmistakable fart. Joe and I were suddenly very awake. Was *that* what we thought it was, a thunderclap from the robes of Father Weber? It was, and though we pinched our noses and received dark stares from our dad, there just is no force on earth strong enough to stop that wildest of laughters: little boys in church laughing when they shouldn't.

Recalling this in the hotel, I eased my dad back down onto the mattress. "You can thank Father Weber for this, Dad. Now go back to sleep."

He turned onto his side, curling his legs up to his chest. Before closing the door behind us I heard him ask, "Now who the devil is Father Weber?"

Later that night we three ventured outside for a few hours, just a safe excursion before returning to the Lake House for one final night's sleep. We walked through the lobby, passing the Fez, whose line of sight never lifted from his polished shoes to acknowledge us. Outside we strolled unbothered toward the promenade running along the Indian Ocean. The sea breeze ran soft fingers through our hair and across our cheeks, carrying with it that sweet scent of the aralia flower, which was in full bloom in trees flanking the broad Galle Road. For a still moment it was as if the city sounds and the beggars were in another room beyond glass. The orange light of the setting sun transformed the ocean into molten copper. The breeze off the ocean that rustled the fronds of the coconut trees carried into our noses the scents of aralia and the sea. This was the Sri Lanka that had enchanted explorers throughout history, and for a brief moment we three Americans shared that experience with them.

And then they were upon us—beggars, kite salesmen, tour guides. Soldiers smoking Marlboros asked for our passports. A boy lured a cobra out of a basket, then insisted we had watched and now owed him ten rupees. Another boy, for the bargain price of five rupees, offered to chase away a rat with his broomstick.

"Stamps!" A barefoot, grizzled man thrust an open book filled with canceled stamps in front of my father's face. "No stamp like Ceylon stamp, my friend. Good gift you take home to Germany. Five hundred rupees but for you my friend only one hundred. The fräulein at home she like."

On our way toward the ocean we crossed Galle Road and then walked across a treeless park with burnt grass called Galle Face Green. The stamp man followed closely, pulled in our gravitational field by my dad's "hmmmm, lovely stamps," and "it's true, my Lil's crazy about stamps."

"Yes, to women Ceylon stamps a rose. They are"—his eyes widened as he brought his face an inch from my father's—"a *love potion.* This I promise."

I steered my dad by the elbow. "C'mon, let's go. Just smile at these jokers and move along."

I could smell the stamp man's acid reek of betel and rum. He turned another page of his book, solemnly. "Only for my good friend do I show my treasure. Look, sir, look at my birds. Ceylon birds most beautiful in world. For you I sell so cheap I no money make but to friend I make most happy. All Germany I make happy. Oktoberfest. Beer. Sausage. I love Germany!"

My father smiled broadly—unnaturally broad, I thought, like a clown's mouth you'd putt into for a free game of miniature golf. Then suddenly his smile disappeared and, patting his stomach-pouch, turned to me and said, "Gotta be careful of thieves. Malone tells me these buggers can sniff out any hiding place. 'John,' he says, 'they'll snatch away your fortune in a hummingbird's heartbeat.' That Malone, he's sure got a way with words."

We watched the sun slip into the sea. In the cooler twilight air the Sri Lankans were emerging from their homes to play on Galle Face

Green: soccer, cricket, children flying tattered kites made from Pop-sicle sticks. Unlike them, dozens of soldiers loitered on the park's perimeter, leaning wearily on their rifles and smoking cigarettes.

The stamp man turned to another page. "If bird stamps my German friend no like I have tigers, peacocks. All cheap. Elephants."

A mother and her five children nudged aside the stamp man and clustered near us, all hands upturned, all faces twisted in grief. Beyond them a few soldiers whistled at Cindy. One soldier put his rifle between his legs and stroked the barrel.

A beggar child tugged on my father's wool pants. "Ooooooh, sir. No food, sir. Five days me no food, sir. Two rupees."

The stamp man pushed away the boy and lifted his book up to my dad. "More stamps, sir. Mangoes, pineapples. Look at papayas. You want to eat stamp."

"One rupee, sir. I hunger."

At the kiss from a beggar girl to the back of his hand, my fa-ther jumped back, retracting his hand beneath his chin. With the other hand he clutched his money pouch. The stamp man, outraged, slapped the girl's face and screamed that no white man should ever be touched. The beggars scattered, and the stamp man, deciding that we were too hard of a sell, drifted out of our orbit and into the more promising one of a Japanese couple.

Beneath the slowly emerging stars the kites still flew, now joined by the black flashes of bats. The moon was nearly full, enabling me to point out to my dad the rabbit image on the moon's surface that recurs throughout Sri Lankan mythology. After searching for a few seconds he said, "All I can make out is the man in the moon," and then looked away from it and from the constellations I told him were never visible in Ohio. Instead, his attention remained earth-bound, asking about the couples sitting beneath umbrellas on the rocks near the sea.

Cindy explained that these were secret lovers avoiding the mar-riages arranged by their parents. "That's how most marriages are still done here, arranged, so if you really do fall in love you have to meet on the sly, like here at night under umbrellas."

"Must be strange," my dad said, "seeing your bride for the first time there at the altar. Suppose she's got a big nose or no teeth, warts or whatever. Sounds like a bit of a crap shoot to me."

"The government cracks down on these love arrangements," I added, "because they say it's against Buddhist teachings. A few years ago some army trucks drove down this sidewalk and fire-hosed all the couples away, like a scene out of Selma."

"They should do it again!" It was the stamp man, books beneath his armpits, stepping between us. "Only better than water next time: Fire! In their faces! Burn up all like devils. That teach. No dirt Ceylon."

My father paid no attention to him. Instead he was looking past the umbrellas down to the surf, down to where three children ran to the ocean, stopped, then retreated in laughter and screams as the waves licked their heels. Further down the beach two men fished while balancing on top of tree trunks stuck fifteen feet out into the surf. Cindy continued to explain why these renegade couples on the rocks were so rare, that in Sri Lanka, honor to the family is so deeply ingrained that you do what the father orders. "You're told to marry someone of your class whom the astrologer says is your match. You get a fat dowry, you stayed married. And those dowries can be a fortune, like fifty thousand rupees, or a house, or a mahogany tree—always from the woman's family."

I told my dad that he should be relieved he had six boys and only one girl. "Think of all the mahogany trees we've saved you."

He didn't respond, nor did he respond when I told him about the ad in the paper offering a tractor as a dowry for a man from a certain class. "Instead of picturing the woman in the ad," I said, "it was the *tractor* that they showed."

His distraction, I realized when I followed his line of sight, was the ocean. At first this thrilled me, supposing my father's mind to be filled with the desire to go swimming with me, the two of us together and alone riding waves for hours just as we had done at Ocean City three decades earlier. Then I saw what my dad was *really* observing. Against the edge of the surf squatted a man, shadowy and grainy in the dying light, scooping up water in his left hand and splashing his underside. When he stood, showing something between his legs that the next wave washed away, my father lightly gasped.

"Jimmy, is that man doing what I think he's doing?"

I didn't know what to say. I knew that my dad must be imagining that this would be his fate, that each day in Sri Lanka he'd have to do his business out in the open. "Don't worry, Dad. You'll always have your privacy—unless, that is, you suddenly have the urge to run to the ocean and drop your drawers."

He wasn't amused. "Malone's gonna hear about this. Why he never told me about this little pleasantry I'll never know."

I decided to lead my dad away from the sea and back to the hotel. We crossed Galle Road, stopping to let pass a tank, an elephant, a bus heavily tilted from overcrowding, and a motorcycle carrying an entire family.

"Will you look at that," my dad said. "Three . . . four . . . *five* on a motorcycle, and three *kids*, and not a one of them wearing a helmet. Maybe I'm old-fashioned but seems to me the government should enforce a helmet law."

"Well, actually, there is a helmet law here," Cindy said. "You see, to *wear* a helmet in Sri Lanka is illegal. Has to do with the JVP, that rebel group we told you about. They tend to ride motorcycles and so the police want to see their faces. Everybody's face, so no helmets are allowed."

My dad, reaching deep inside his pocket for his rosary, just shook his head and said he was getting a bit hungry. Cindy and I conferred in Sinhala about the best place to take him. She suggested a swanky

Western hotel for one last familiar meal; I insisted on a local dive we knew about, one of the common, grimy diners called *kadee*s.

"It's up to you," she said. "He's your father, but just remember how old he is."

When my dad asked what we were talking about, I just told him to watch out for the traffic and to follow us.

Cindy and I entered the *kadee* first. Lingering a few steps behind was my seventy-four-year-old father, no doubt leery of his first immersion into the Third World. He watched a soldier light his cigarette from the strand of rope hanging out front, a rope that would burn slowly all day just for this purpose. Then my dad stepped into the doorway of the bleak little restaurant, its interior dimly lit by three hissing kerosene lamps. The walls were mud, and I wondered if my dad half-expected to see cave paintings of buffalo on them.

There were no women inside. In a corner beneath a Buddha shrine sat five soldiers smoking Marlboros, each hardly aware of the machine guns resting across their laps. One soldier with his boots on the table threw a handful of rice at the waiter's head. Another soldier, seeing three white foreigners entering a place where few white foreigners had ever entered, stood and blew a stream of snot onto the restaurant floor. A dog loped out from the darkness to sniff it.

I saw my dad rapidly moving his lips, and when I heard the light clacking of rosary beads in his pocket, I knew he was praying. Cindy led him by the arm to a table. The waiter, barefoot and sullen, wiped away the mess on the table with the edge of his hand, but the rice falling from his hair kept replenishing the kernels he had scattered onto the floor. One of the soldiers yelled at the waiter for more cigarettes, prompting him to trot away as if we didn't exist. My dad noticed the grimy bottoms of the waiter's feet. He noticed a dog, its hide scratched raw from lice, rooting around near our legs. He noticed the ants gathering on our table, and he looked up to notice the sweat glazed on my face. I heard the clatter of his rosary quicken, and as he prayed, I prayed too—prayed that of all the things my old father was noticing on his second day outside America, the rat flashing across the ceiling beam wouldn't be one of them.

"You'll love the food here, Dad," I said. "Real authentic."

He looked away from me and up to the kerosene lamp, hissing above our heads. Its light pulsated as if it were breathing, as if its twin gauzy mantles were the lungs of a transparent animal. The waiter, who had not yet taken our order, went from lamp to lamp pouring in kerosene—not because they needed it, but because a soldier, with his machine gun leveled at the waiter's navel and saying, "Rat-a-tat-tat-tat-tat-tat," had ordered him to do so. We three leaned back far in our chairs when he attended to the lamp above us, afraid that it would suddenly explode. But it didn't, and because it didn't none of us minded the puddle of kerosene the waiter had left behind on our table.

My father sat with his arms on his lap. His breath passed only through his nose. He flinched at a mosquito orbiting his head and then kicked aside a dog sniffing his wing tips.

"You kids come here much?" he asked.

Before I could answer, a soldier from the corner table threw a beer bottle near our feet. My father jerked and then, with his elbows cupped in his palms, began to rock slightly. We turned to the sound of a chair in the corner toppling over. There a soldier stood, then stretched, then tugged at his crotch in the direction of Cindy. He joked for a while with his buddies, then walked slowly toward our table, his boots tromping thick and defiant on the cracked wood floor, his machine gun clattering against the bullets strapped to his belt. The kerosene light that pulsed and hissed lit up the soldier's face above us, and what we saw for the first time beneath his war costume terrified us even more: This was just a boy, a boy who had bypassed childhood and who now lived in a boy's fantasy world where he is

44

all-powerful and can invent the rules. And I wondered: Could he or any of the other four menchildren in the corner sitting beneath the statue of Buddha distinguish between boyhood games of hide-'n-go-seek and this deadly game of war they each held in their laps?

The soldier above us didn't move. He leered long and openly at Cindy, whose body inclined toward mine as if her very timid husband had the courage to protect her. Without moving his stare from Cindy, the soldier blew smoke into my face. I did nothing except close my eyes. In the corner his mates whooped and raised their machine guns, and to me this whole scene was descending into a nightmare in which we three whites would soon be forced at gunpoint to lick a boot.

Suddenly the soldier tired of us and moved on to another target. Against the front counter leaned a cardboard Kodak display, a life-sized white woman in a red bathing suit, her prominent breasts uplifted. In Sri Lanka, where the women are nearly mummified head to toe by six yards of cloth, an ad such as this, conceived twelve thousand miles away in Rochester, New York, certainly worked to get the attention of Sri Lankan men. The attention was so strong, in fact, that the cardboard bathing suit in nearly every one of these posters I had seen throughout Sri Lanka had been scratched away at the crotch or peeled upwards. The soldier in this *kadee*, urged on by the other boy soldiers, grabbed what remained of her red suit and shredded it upwards from crotch to throat as if disemboweling an animal.

Cindy shuddered. I looked away. My dad moved onto another decade of his rosary beads. And then, with the kerosene lamp hissing, the soldier dropped to one knee and licked the cardboard with a darting tongue. The soldiers in the corner clamored for more.

We left the *kadee* without eating.

In the taxi to the hotel the only words spoken were Cindy's directions in Sinhala to the driver. Later, the three of us went to bed in the same hotel room with fists of hunger in our stomachs.

45

Cindy fell asleep next to me, the smell of kerosene still in her hair. For a long time I stayed awake with one eye staring sideways at my father. He was sitting on the edge of his bed in his pajamas, murmuring prayers in time with his rosary beads, his shoulders curled around his face.

I closed my eyelids to block out the guilt, hoping to conjure up scenes of baseball games and barbecues. Instead, what played on the underside of my lids was a ghastly movie—of Cindy as an eviscerated Kodak model, of the soldiers with lit Marlboros dousing my face in kerosene. In time I opened my eyes from these horrors, and there still sitting on the edge of his bed was my father, praying.

And so it would remain for the next hour, and for every hour after that until the gray light of dawn would offer to awaken us both from our darkness.

**4**

The next morning I woke up hungry and smelling of kerosene. I rolled over to see if my dad had fled in the night to America, leaving behind a note: "Too old for this, Jimmy. Want my bacon and eggs and Lil. Left twenty bucks behind for you kids."

But he was there, fully dressed and standing in front of the mirror, looping one end of his tie over the other. He splashed Old Spice on both cheeks and, noticing I was awake, turned and said, "It's Sunday, Jimmy. You remember what we do on Sunday, don't you?"

That explained it. Leave it to the Catholic Church to get my dad's mind back onto comfortable ground. "Oh sure, Dad, sure," I replied, far too eager to do anything for him after the calamity of the night before. If the man wants a Mass, the man gets a Mass. So what if I rarely went myself. He had attended Mass on over thirty-eight hundred consecutive Sundays spanning nine decades, and I was happy to join him now as if continuing my own streak. I dressed in a good mood. "Dad," I said, "mind if I borrow a bit of your Old Spice?" and while slapping myself joked about how the priests ought to use my mom's chocolate-chip cookies as communion hosts. My dad glowered at me.

"The host," he said, "is nothing to joke about."

I slapped myself again, the old-man smell of Old Spice now thick in the room. But not thick enough. There was still the unmistakable smell of kerosene, alive and black, now bringing with it the vapor of those boy soldiers and that Kodak girl, all snarling at us in the mirror. My dad, Cindy, myself—we all felt it, I knew, by the way we busied ourselves and the way we avoided eye contact and the way we hurried out of the room. Through it all we dealt with the trauma the way all Toner traumas were handled: We never spoke about it.

Downstairs in the lobby I asked the Fez to whistle a taxi for us, guessing that doormen in high places still did such things. My plan was to accept a little leisure this morning—a cab to the church, then a cab to the train station to catch the 11:02, then a first-class air-conditioned train ride with big windows—before arriving at my friend Vijay's primitive house on a remote tea estate. "I grieve," said the Fez. "It is my distasteful but necessary task to inform Sir and Son of Sir, and"—he bowed to Cindy—"pulchritudinous Daughter of Sir that there are no taxis. Not today. Problems abound in fair isle of Serendib. No taxis, no buses. Transport for the day must be of the elemental ilk, that of the foot."

"What's the problem?" I asked. "Is there a JVP curfew?"

At the mention of "JVP" the Fez looked around nervously, then whispered, "With duest of respects, the utterance of those initials by the Sir is with considerable peril. We are a lovely family, we of Serendib, and like all families we have our problems, our tiffs. My lachrymose glands shed at the thought. No taxis, no buses. Outside Colombo, perhaps. Inside Colombo for one week our humble citizens must locomote on God's twin gifts."

And so we walked. Cindy led, striding her purposeful Nordic stride well ahead of us, while I followed, pulling my dad's suitcase on its little rubber wheels through all the deep craters in the sidewalk. It toppled over every few seconds. In front of me I could see the sweat already beading on my dad's neck, even though it wasn't yet

8 A.M. After a few hundred yards he stopped, sighed the kind of deep sigh that I imagine precedes death, and then gulped so deeply from Big Green the Gatorade bottle that his Indians cap fell off. He squinted into the rays of sunlight piercing through the coconut fronds like swords.

He unzipped the little backpack my mother had bought for him at K-Mart. "Where's that damn umbrella? Malone told me, 'Stay in the shade or make your own. Or you die.'" He unsheathed the white collapsible Totes umbrella from its plastic tube and opened it. "Never been so damn hot in all my life."

I told my dad that he looked like a mushroom with that umbrella open.

He shot me a harsh look. "The heat worries me, Jimmy. Now how far's this church, anyway?"

"Not far."

"What's your idea of 'not far'?"

"Not far at all."

He moaned and kept walking. His untied laces clicked lightly on the street, which we had moved onto because the sidewalk craters had become too deep. Each of his steps imprinted the soles of his wing tips in the soft asphalt, and from behind I laughed quietly at the image of my father stuck like a brontosaurus in a tar pit. I imagined future archaeologists on their knees, dusting off a skeleton still clutching a green Gatorade bottle and a Totes umbrella.

My dad turned to me, his face wrinkled toward his nose. "Is there a joke I'm missing?"

"A joke?"

"You were laughing. Could you let me in on your little joke?"

"I wasn't laughing."

He walked on, his stride heavy and plodding. He didn't tip his cap to the woman sweeping the front of her store. He held his handkerchief over his nose while passing the man waving incense around the entrance to his shop. With his white Totes he swatted away a stray dog. And when an elephant chained at the ankles passed us going the other way, my dad never bothered to look up.

At the sight of the church my father's pace quickened. In running toward it he was running away from this alien, dangerous Sri Lankan world he had briefly experienced, and running toward the known. Here was the familiar, including the four nuns on the church steps wearing the same head-to-toe black habits he had seen his whole life.

"Sisters! My good Sisters!" my dad shouted, confident that in and around a Catholic church, English is the only language. With sudden energy he ran up the steps with his hand outstretched. "John Toner, Sisters. Cleveland, Ohio. Near Chicago, if that helps any. Say, Sisters, I'm here visiting my son Jimmy and his wife, both in the Peace Corps, over here to do . . . Say, Jimmy, what is it you're doing over here?"

I was ten yards away, dragging his suitcase as if it were part of a penance. "C'mon, Dad," I growled. "Do I really have to tell you again that—"

"Say, Sister, how many nuns in your order?"

"Fifty," she answered. When I came alongside them I could see a long hair growing like a spider leg from a mole in her chin, and I wanted to reach up and yank it. "We expect seventy this year, God willing."

My dad's eyes widened. "Seventy! That's fantastic, Sister. Jeez, what we'd give in my big parish for five. You see, nowadays the ladies in America don't go much for the convent."

"Pity."

"I'll say it's a pity. Who's left to teach our children but the lay, and I'm here to tell you that they cost a bundle."

"Pity."

While they gabbed on and on like long-separated friends, I pointed out the mole and spider hair to Cindy. "Go pluck it out," I whispered, "and I'll give you a cookie." I was nearly serious because it was bringing back such bad memories of my third-grade teacher, Sister Marstella. She used to torment students, especially Sue Finley, who always froze up and burst into tears when faced with a math problem at the board. Sister Marstella, blessed with a mole hair sprouting from her chin, would fly into a rage at this whimpering child. "Finley," she'd scream, twining the hair around her finger, "don't you dare get my floors wet! Go get the bucket!" And so she would, bringing the bucket out from the closet and setting it in front of the class. "Now, cry all you want, Finley. Go right ahead and cry, just as long as you don't get a drop on my floors."

By this time the parish priest had met my father. They were chatting away like great pals, laughing, frequently touching each other's arms and shoulders.

"Jimmy. Jimmy and Cindy. Let me introduce you to Father . . . to Father . . ."

"Gunatilika. Father Nimal Gunatilika, but my good friends like you they call me 'Nimal' or 'Nimmy' or sometimes"—his head shot back in a roar—"they call me things I don't care to repeat."

I was amazed that this bad joke had made its way around the world. I shook his hand, a soft and puffy hand limited in its lifetime to turning Bible pages and placing hosts on tongues. I wanted a closer look at his thumb, wondering if it was polished and indented from the friction of a million tongues.

My dad placed his hand on the small of the priest's back. "Kids, my friend Father Nimal"—friend?—"has just been telling me about his wonderful project at St. Patrick's. A genuine boy's band."

The priest nodded, the sun glinting across his well-oiled hair. "Many prizes we win."

"That's right," my dad said. "And he tells me that the only thing missing is a saxophone."

"It will give us the song of angels."

"Nothing quite like a saxophone, Father Nimal."

"An *alto* saxophone. Not just any saxophone. Alto. It will give us sound like thunder across your American plains."

"That would be a marvelous sound, Father," my dad smiled. "Give me a week or two back in Cleveland and we'll see if we can't rustle up some thunder to send on over here."

I couldn't believe my ears. Here in Sri Lanka, a country without rabies vaccine or penicillin, a country of underfed babies and beggars rummaging the streets, a country in which a war was wiping out entire villages and creating over a million refugees—that into this dire country my father would be sending a saxophone.

"Dad," I said, "an alto sax is really not—"

"Two," Father Nimal interrupted. "We could really use two. Two to give us stereo thunder. The omnipresent angels, and all that."

My dad held the priest's elbow. "Then two it'll be. You know, at one of our high schools, St. Ignatius, I bet I could dig up a couple of saxes just sitting around in the basement collecting dust. You know, they practically *throw* away their instruments in that joint."

"Ah, yes," Father Nimal nodded. "Yours is a land of plenty."

The bells for Mass rang, shifting Father Nimal's expression from dreaminess to irritation. I supposed he was worried that this little intrusion called a Mass would interfere with his cutting the sax deal.

"John," the priest said, "my good good friend John. We *must* meet after I do my duty. We meet on this spot. Hah-hah, 'Johnny on the spot,' I believe you say. Immediately after Mass we meet and continue our friendship. Our good and lasting friendship. No ocean shall us two part."

I smiled my phony smile, then turned and whispered to Cindy, "Can you believe it: alto saxes. You know, that's what the JVP have been fighting for all along. Give them a crate of altos and that's the end of the war."

"Come to the front," Father Nimal said. "I provide for my best friends the best pew as befits celebrities. The best view in house." My dad declined, saying that out of humility he'd prefer to sit with the "regular" folk. "Very well, then. I meet you right here on the spot—soon! soon! very very soon!—and we continue our discussion. See you later . . . alligator!"

His guffaw echoed throughout the church.

We three whites entered the church—one with enthusiasm, two others with resignation. Once inside this dim and familiar place my father's posture straightened up. Here at glorious last was his refuge. The language, the customs, when to kneel, when and how to triple-bless oneself before the Gospel is read—the man knew it all. He smiled his broad jack-o'-lantern smile, the beggars and menacing soldiers of the last forty-eight hours now just shadows, the toilets and snakes and mystery son of the next six hundred and fifty hours now just vague concerns. Where there had been kerosene fumes, now there was incense. Where there had been men defecating into the ocean and Koreans screeching in elevators, now there were candles and an altar, crosses and confessionals.

We sidled into our pew. A hundred black faces stared at us, we three towering pillars. I pitied the people directly behind us who would now have to worship into the small of our backs. I turned to apologize to them for our bulk through some universal gesture—a shrug, a smirk—but in response they all just smiled enthusiastically at me. I wondered if they knew we were the alto-sax benefactors.

My dad turned to whisper to me. "Just think, Jimmy. At this very moment around the world a billion people, of all languages and colors, are doing the same thing: praying in a Catholic church."

And at least half of those billion, I thought, are little kids wishing they were somewhere else: throwing a tennis ball against the side of a garage, or stretched on the floor watching the Yankees coming to bat, or eating a bowl of Frosted Flakes. Half a billion kids with hair too short and with clothes too stiff, all thinking the same thing: Enough! Enough of this madness, enough of this tomb. Let me run outside. Let me slide head-first into second base just ahead of the catcher's throw.

Father Nimal entered. To his side were two altar boys, barefoot. I whispered to Cindy about my days as an altar boy, when we'd ring the bells at the wrong time on purpose, when we'd let the incense fly out of its chamber and set the carpet on fire. One time we found in the priest's closet a stack of pornographic books, including the only title I remembered, *Breaking the Habit*, about nuns who doubled as prostitutes.

"Shhhh!" my dad snapped at us. "We're in church!"

In front on the altar Father Nimal widened his arms. *Let us pray, my sisters and brothers,* he said in Sinhala.

For a little while I tried to squish tight my eyelids like my pious dad, thinking that this small action alone would unlock the mysteries of Catholicism. In a minute, though, seeing nothing but sea horses gliding across the backs of my lids, I gave up and opened my eyes. I saw that in our half of the church were only men, barefoot, wrapped in sarongs, their one and only "dress" shirt thin as gauze and neatly pressed by irons heated with coals. Of the ten watches I could see, each told a different time. Across the aisle stood the women with white doilies crowning their heads. This matter of doilies, now as outdated in America as the fish-on-Friday routine, fascinated me as a kid. I once tried on my mother's doily in the secrecy of her closet, bobby-pinning it to my crewcut. Recalling this in the Sri Lankan church, I wondered if that doily action classified me as some kind of child transvestite.

These were not holy thoughts. I looked over at my father, his eyelids clamped tight in prayer, and vowed that on his behalf I would get *something* holy out of this Mass: I will, I will, I will. But weak of will is all I am, and as my yawns widened and my spine sagged I had

54

to tap my daydream reserves to get me through this tedium: There he is, Jim Toner, completing seventeen passes in a row to bring a football championship to Cleveland! All hail Jim Toner, our hero! And oh yes, all you nubile young ladies waiting outside the locker room door for just a glimpse! Oh yes, my bodyguards, you may allow Sheila Hart in her short shorts to come join me while I'm in the whirlpool and—"

*All kneel!* Father Nimal ordered. *All pray to our Lord Jesus Christ!*

I knelt, the sharp wood grinding into my knees like a well-deserved punishment. But Father Nimal droned, and droned, and before long there I was, back to pass—complete!—for my fourth touchdown in twelve minutes. The TV cameras switch to Sheila in the stands, her knuckles in her mouth, not sure what her man has just done but not really caring because she loves him unconditionally.

*. . . and when Jesus died on the cross for our sins, the nails driven deep into his palms, the pain . . .*

My butt had slouched down to rest on the edge of the pew. Next to me knelt my father, forty years my senior, his back ramrod straight as a Marine drill sergeant. He still clenched tight his eyelids, sealing in sacred thoughts that never drifted to football heroics and a breathless Sheila. Or did they? Maybe, just maybe, my dad is a pervert after all! Maybe on the dark screen of his eyelids he is picturing Betty Grable blowing bath bubbles onto him, purring, while in the next room near the chilled champagne the turntable plays "Stardust."

*Please stand to worship the Lord.*

I stood with vigor, my back as solid and erect as an alto sax. I said the "Our Father" with vigor. And with vigor I turned to my father for the "kiss of peace," that part of the Mass in which you mumble something about peace to your neighbors while shaking their hands, all the time worried that your palms are too sweaty. In hip America the handshake can be a hug, an option which my father, always keen for contact under the ruse of prayer, fully exploited. After shaking those black hands around us, my dad and I faced each other—me his Betty, he my Sheila—and hugged what would have been a meaningful, emotional hug except for one thing: He patted my back with quick light fluttering taps. Phony taps.

At communion time the Sri Lankans rushed the altar as if they were boarding the last bus for the night. They knelt at the altar railing instead of receiving the communion host standing up, American-style. My dad waited patiently for an opening until I pushed him into a crack. A few feet down the line I wedged between Cindy and another woman, who reeked of coconut oil in her hair. While kneeling there in the most solemn part of this ritual, my mind naturally turned to the subject of tongues. I asked Cindy in a whisper if she thought the priest noticed tongue textures: smooth, bumpy, curdled.

She and my dad both told me to be quiet.

We waited. While waiting I wondered if priest school had a course on tongue anatomy, its textbook filled with glossy pictures of world tongues. I asked Cindy, "Do you think priest schools have a dummy tongue? You know, one they can practice on to get the placement just right—not too far back for fear of choking, not too far forward or it'll fall off?"

"Jimmy!" my dad hissed. "Enough is enough!"

Father Nimal approached us. The altar boy shadowed the priest with the gold paten to catch any communion hosts that might dribble off a chin. As an altar boy I loved holding the paten. I used to hold it solemnly against old necks that sagged and new necks taut as dolphin flesh. Against Sheila Hart's neck—it was no mere neck, this flesh of the gods—yes, against her sacred skin my paten drooped and drooped until the priest, with a whack, straightened me up. Against other classmates' necks I had more control. Whenever George Donnelly flipped out his tongue, I would tap the knife-edge of the paten against his Adam's apple.

56

Once, lancing him at just the precise moment on just the precise spot (altar boys know neck anatomy well), he spit out the host onto the priest's vestment.

"Sorry, Father," George covered for me. "Just can't seem to shake this cough."

I held the paten beneath a few thousand lolling tongues in my childhood, just waiting, like a rural fireman, for that one moment of catastrophe to justify all this caution. Then one day it happened: A host fell.

And I missed.

I remember in slow motion the host hitting the edge of the paten, bouncing across the plate with a thin "ting" before falling, with snowflake softness, into a puddle of slush dragged in on galoshes. The priest froze. Together in horror we watched the Body of Christ dissolve in sludge.

Later in the back room he collared me. "That host," the priest trembled, his Irish face red with drink and fury, "is the *Lord!* The Lord our God, Mr. Toner! You let fall the body of Our Lord Jesus Christ, the body that died for our sins—your sins! your *many* sins, Mr. Toner!" (I thought about interrupting him to ask about the plot of *Breaking the Habit.*) "The body that hung for hours with nails in his palms when you, YOU!, would scream about a little bitty staple in your finger!"

*The Body of Christ.*

I lifted my eyes to see Father Nimal holding a host above me. And then I saw it, the paten, ominous as a guillotine, nearing my tender throat. Was that a puddle of slush jiggling on the paten? Was that a hood over the altar boy's head?

Fortunately, mine is an ugly tongue, bumpy and milky, a slice of lunar surface in my mouth. At its sight the altar boy retracted the paten, risking a falling host but sparing my jugular. I could feel Father Nimal's thumb hit my tongue, and I wondered: How many organisms have just invaded my body?

With host in mouth and not a sacred thought in my mind, I rose from the railing, my place taken by a rush of people. On my way up the aisle I didn't know whether to look pious, to look for pretty faces, or to just stick out my tongue to shock everybody.

I slid into my pew, and I tried to pray: "Dear God, to whom I never pray but I'll give it a shot. Please improve my father's posture. Please get that Korean lady to chill out a little bit. Please give Cleveland a baseball championship before I die. And please thin out all Sri Lankan buses so my dad can ride in luxury, reclining in a La-Z-Boy chair. Amen. Oh, and if you're up to it, help my dad and me get through this Sri Lanka thing. Amen again."

Once outside the church in the glorious steamy tropical air I wanted something as a reward for enduring Mass: a touch football game, some pancakes, a rerun of *I Dream of Jeannie*.

Instead I retrieved my dad's suitcase, yanking it behind me like a tired old dog. A crowd of Sri Lankans swarmed around us, moving us down to the road in their current. From somewhere behind us a voice was screaming, *Stop! Stop the white man!*

It was Father Nimal, his arms waving and his neck stretching to find us. *You must stop the white man! Alto sax! Tell my friend the white man to send the sax. Two! Stereo thunder like the plains. He must not forget.*

The words "alto sax" rippled through the crowd, a hundred black faces repeating "alto sax, alto sax, alto sax" nonstop during our remaining walk to the train station. Little by little the jack-o'-lantern grin left my father's face—my slouching father, my father dripping sweat beneath a white Totes umbrella.

His last sanctuary was behind him, and I think he knew it.

On the platform at the train station twenty minutes later I was not loved. My father sat in one corner, panting, his shirt saturated and his Totes drooping and his face overcome with gloom, while in the other corner sat Cindy with her arms crossed and her eyes focused on her toe. Between my dad and her were many other plastic chairs, all orange and empty. There was no one else on the platform.

"It's gone," Cindy said to her toe. "An hour ago."

I was astonished. "That can't be. I checked the schedule—"

"It's gone." She tightened the grip around her ribs. "And there aren't any more trains for the day. Maybe for a couple of days."

The sun pressed down on my head. I looked both ways down the track, hoping to conjure up a train. "Listen, Cindy, I checked and rechecked that—"

"It's gone." She looped one leg over the other, bobbing it up and down. "Why we didn't get here earlier is beyond me or why you didn't *ask* someone is beyond me instead of relying on that ancient train book—"

"Ancient! It's new! It's a month old!"

"It's printed in Sri Lanka, Jim, not Switzerland." At times like this she thrust that "Jim" at me like a bayonet. "So now you can go tell your father what it means to not have a train around here. Go on. Go tell him about the glories of bus travel."

I looked toward him at the other end, a rosary entwined around his fingers, but my mind rested not on him but on all the chairs in between. I counted them: eighty-four. All plastic, all bright orange, all broad in the seat to accommodate the full range of the world's butts. I had seen these exact same chairs throughout my life. I remembered in my high-school cafeteria playing human shuffleboard with these orange chairs. Billy Coughlin, half our weight and fully agreeable, sat on one of these orange, broad-seated chairs that I would push toward the speckled square tile twenty yards away. We competed for bags of Fritos.

"Who do you suppose has the world commission on these chairs?" I asked Cindy. "I swear they're ubiquitous. They're everywhere."

She looked up from her toe to me, regarding my face as if I were some mold in the back of the refrigerator. "I know what 'ubiquitous' means. And what the hell are you talking about, anyhow?"

A door shut loudly behind us. It was the stationmaster walking toward the exit, a heavy bracelet of keys clanking around his wrist. I ran over to him, flipping through my travel book for the page of train schedules. I lost the page when I swatted half a dozen flies orbiting my head. Finding it again, I called to the stationmaster in Sinhala, *Sir. Just a minute, sir. Where's the train, the 11:02 to Patana? See, it says right here: 11:02 to Patana.*

He disregarded the book. "There is no error," he said in English, and walked on.

The keys rattled when I grabbed his wrist. "Look. Look right here. It says—"

"You should not use such an outdated book, my friend. Now if you'll please let me go—"

"Outdated!" I laughed, arching my eyebrows. "Take a look at the date: April 1 to May 10. This doesn't expire for another two weeks. For two more weeks there's a train coming at 11:02 to take my very old father—do you see him over there, the old and respected man? He's a judge, and he expects to take the 11:02 to Patana." The patches of hair shooting out of the stationmaster's ears were bothering me, as were the flies landing on my face and not on his. "I suggest you get back in your office and prepare for the train."

He twirled the bracelet of keys around his wrist. "Things," he smiled, "can change very quickly in my country. Overnight sometimes. Confirm. You must always confirm. Leave nothing to chance. Maybe Sri Lanka is not the place for you and your father."

He left me alone on the platform with eighty-four orange plastic chairs and two people who, I think, would have liked to see an elephant squash me. I stared down the tracks, certain that the

mirage of rising heat was an empty train full of sofas just for us. A
fly landed on my cheek, and I left it alone. I looked at Cindy and
then quickly away when I felt her eyes burning into mine. And
I wondered: What fate is worse, my head covered with flies or a
wild-eyed wife?

Across the platform I could feel more wild eyes, my father's.
"No train!" I imagined him thinking. "Are you telling me, Jim,
that your seventy-four-year-old wheezing father—your *father!* don't
forget I'm your *father!*—that I have to leave this shade and trudge
on in this . . . this sauna! Don't get me stuck in tar, son. Don't let
me die a death in tar."

I needed a basset hound right about then. And a cookie.

An hour later my father sat at a bus stop in the shade of a palm tree
near a couple of cows nibbling on lemon grass. Cindy and I stood
in a long and static line, our shoulders drooping from the weight
of the sun. We cast no shadow. The few people walking through
town clung to the shade of the overhanging awnings.

"Where's the Yukon when you need it?" I said to no one.

Most of the others in line stared at the comical sight of my
father: Totes in one hand, rosary in the other, an empty Big Green
at his feet. A dog sniffed his wing tips.

None of us were very much alive.

When word reached us that the bus would be an hour late, maybe
two, Cindy and I left the line to sit next to my father. For a long
time nobody said anything or did anything. Then, reaching into his
backpack, my dad said, "Anybody up for a game of hearts?"

I wasn't. He asked if I'd rather play gin rummy but I just stood
and walked over to the coconut man. I bought a couple of coconuts with the crowns hacked off, drank the water inside of one and
then, after my dad cited scientific evidence from Malone about the

diseases floating in coconut juice, gave the other to Cindy. My dad ran his tongue across his lips.

Two hours later there was still no sign of a bus. Eventually we walked back to the Lake House by the same route we had covered that morning, the sun now so low that my dad didn't need his Totes. We passed the church, we passed the man with incense closing up his shop, and when we entered the lobby of the Lake House, the Fez stayed seated and turned a shoulder to us.

# 5

The next morning we stood for two hours waiting for the bus. It arrived, tilting heavily from all the bodies hanging out the door, kicking up dust that swirled around the twenty of us running to reach the door. No one got off and yet all of us, with the bus still moving, managed to crush ourselves on board. My father, clutching his money pouch, was somehow swallowed up into the interior through the narrowest of slits; Cindy and I became part of the throng hanging outside the door with only a foot, or a few toes of that foot, on the edge of a step.

The bus labored away. With each mangled shift of gears a new plume of black exhaust came spiraling up through the rear window and into the bus. No one seemed to mind. In the middle stood my father, looking bewildered and lost, his arms straight-jacketed against his sides. He couldn't raise his arms to wipe the sweat trickling down his forehead, down his cheeks, and down onto the head of a woman standing beneath him. He swayed and pitched with the roll of the bus, his fingers gripping the center pole like the mast of a ship in a typhoon. He looked funny to me. His entire head and baseball cap rose above the crowd of black faces, and to me it appeared as if this head, lopped off, was a trophy that the natives were carrying back to their king.

Eventually Cindy and I wiggled inside the bus, claimed a seat up front for my dad and then stood in the back. His was the worst seat. I could see his face pressed against the windshield and his knees tucked up high to his chin. He shared the seat with two others, one a turbaned man holding up a crate of chickens for the white man's approval. My dad nodded politely at the chickens and then turned to watch the world passing outside. And I wondered: What in my dad's life had prepared him for this? Where in Cleveland are there live chickens, turbans, thick exhaust, dashboards with Buddha statuettes? Where are there buses barreling along cliff sides without guardrails or rocketing through towns at runaway speeds? What sense can he make of the elephants walking nonchalantly down the street, or the men in roadside shops pedaling on their sewing machines?

But at least he had a seat. I had to stand for three hours, gripping the overhead luggage racks in a pose of crucifixion. People crushed against every part of my body, even into the hollow of my armpits. Meanwhile, Cindy had scored a seat nearby and was making odd, elastic faces at the baby held next to her. I envied that baby, that well-fed, seated, coddled baby. Instead I stood hour after hour, sweaty and miserable, and though I tried to fantasize my way through this journey—repairing the roof of my igloo, hitting a grand slam, giggling with Sheila Hart in a convertible—I kept returning to the heat and to the fatigue, to the utter insanity of humans agreeing to travel in this way.

Midway to Vijay's home in Patana the bus stopped for more passengers. They squished in tighter against my ribs, and at the moment when I thought that God ought to be smacked around with an alto sax, I heard her.

"Git in now! I say git git git and don't be shy. This is no time to be shy and oh for the sake of Jesus stop your squealing and *git in!*" Then she saw us. "Jeeyim! Ciiiiiindy! Lordy lordy if the sun ain't shining on the head of Miss Jewel E. Jewel today!"

That was her real name: Jewel E. Jewel, 65, a Peace Corps volunteer from Arkansas. She wasn't your typical Peace Corps volunteer. Jewel E. Jewel—fond of drink, her fingers stained yellow from chain smoking, her face creased as a walnut—fit more neatly into the mold of bricklayers and tugboat captains than into the mold of Peace Corps English teachers. This became most apparent to me when I observed her teaching.

"You!" she shouted, pointing her yellow finger at a Sri Lankan student. "You git on up on your feet and talk me a little English and no excuses."

A terrified young woman half-stood, half-sat. "I beg your pardon, Miss Jewel?"

"Up up up I say! Wax done clog up dem goddamned big brown ears of yours?"

"I beg your pardon, Miss Jewel?"

She smoked, she drank, she cussed, she carried a bowie knife ("my Arkansas toothpick"), and she couldn't teach a lick or speak a word of Sinhala, but she did one thing right: She stayed. While our Peace Corps ranks dwindled from thirty-six to five because of the war, while the bombings and the idleness prompted the Peace Corps office in Washington to provide us with psychiatric help, Jewel E. Jewel kept wondering what all the fuss was about. "I ain't leaving even if they fire a load of buckshot into my be-hind. And anyone who does up and leave is a yeller-bellied fool. Now how's about crackin' open a beer for Miss Jewel E. Jewel."

On this day she boarded the bus fresh from a trip back to America, financed by a little illegal gem running. One of the ironies of Jewel E. Jewel was that she was stationed in the jewel capital of Sri Lanka, Ratnapura. On our bus she squirmed her way through a solid block of people—"Comin' on through, little people. Make room for Miss Jewel E. Jewel"—while balancing a large package on her head. After she got settled I asked her what she was carrying.

"Brassieres!" she hollered. "Nothin' but big brassieres, 44 on up. Jim dear, you listen to Miss Jewel: These little brown ladies just love their brassieres. Love 'em. And let me tell you that J.C. Penney—have you been to Penney's lately, honey? Let me tell you, it's a place of quality. Cheryl Tiegs brassieres, that's the kind of quality you'll find at J.C. Penney nowadays. I got me a whole passel of these here brassieres, the biggest they got. I says to the manager, 'Gimme 'em big, honey, biggest in the state.' And here they be, three dozen for my village ladies. Oh lordy lordy they'll just color pink over them."

By this time every passenger on the bus had turned toward Jewel, all trying to make sense of a voice that to them must have sounded like a sitar out of tune.

"The boobs in this here country," she continued, "are the mightiest in the world. That's a goddamned fact. Ask little Cindy. Women notice. And it's time these big brown boobs got"—she paused to cackle, raspy from heavy smoking—"a little American support! Say, Cindy sweetheart, be a dear and light me up this cigarette. Just open up that winder and get me goin'." Cindy ignored her, which was an improvement over the contempt she usually showed Jewel. Unfazed, Jewel turned to me. "Jim dear, did I tell you these brassieres were free? That's F-R-E-E. Every one a them a gift when I told the manager—oh, lordy, I was wearing my flirtin' shoes that day!—when I told him I am a woman of service over here. 'I serves the people and the Lord in no particular order,' I tells him. Jimmy dear, let it be known that J.C. Penney has a goddamned big heart. And Cheryl Tiegs sure gives 'em the stamp of quality."

For no apparent reason the bus suddenly stopped. I looked out the window through the thicket of arms holding onto the rail and saw five army jeeps at a checkpoint. A soldier from somewhere outside ordered everybody off the bus, quickly, more quickly. I called to my father, whose knees were still pressed to his chin, to leave his bags on the bus and exit with all the others.

Once outside I introduced Jewel to my dad. "My oh my," she said, shaking his hand and not letting go, "they sure do make the fellers handsome up there in Ohio."

My dad said that he didn't quite catch her name.

"Miss Jewel E. Jewel," she said, throwing back her shoulders, "from Arkansas, the only self-sufficient state in the Union. My oh my if I'd a known I'd be meetin' a judge today, I'd a done somethin' about these yeller trousers." She twisted at the hips to show us the seat of her pants. "Back there at the bus stop I was waitin' and waitin' with these big brassieres on top of my head and, well, I just needed to sits down right then and there to recollect myself. So I sits and if God in glorious heaven ain't my witness, I sits square on a dozen eggs! Square on 'em, splat-like, yolks and all! You folks'll just have to forgive my yeller pants."

My dad squinted at her as if reading a sign from a great distance.

"Judge, you got a light for a lady?" She handed my dad her lighter. "This modern feminine shit is for the birds, ain't that right, Judge? You can open a door for me any time, light my cigarette any time, buy me a cocktail any time. Any ol' time." Cindy shot her a burning look. "You married, Judge?"

"My Lil, she—"

"She's a lucky lady is what she is. And the only way to keep a lucky lady is to buy her a gem. Tell 'em the truth, Cindy. We ladies go to jelly when it comes to this gem shit."

"Oh please," Cindy said. "Can't you find some other sucker to sell your gems to?"

Jewel exhaled her smoke. "I do believe I was addressing your elder, little girl."

"Well," my dad said, "Lil did ask me to bring her one of those blue sapphires. Seems that Malone got his Peggy a big one and ever since she sticks it under my Lil's nose."

"Can't have none of that, Judge. If it's a sapeer you want then it's a sapeer you'll get." This was Jewel up to her old tricks, steering

Westerners to her gem dealer, who then gave her a big cut. "You come to me and we'll fix your Lilly up nice and tidy."

"Shut up!" a soldier yelled, striding toward us. "No talk. Passport. Give."

"My oh my," Jewel said to him. "Were you absent from class when God gave out manners?"

"Shut mouth!"

My dad handed his passport to the soldier, whose rifle was leveled at my navel. He inspected the passport without humor, glancing from the photo to the face and back to the photo. My dad smiled, reaching to tip his Indians cap until he realized it was back on the bus.

The soldier nodded my dad over to the other line and then examined Jewel's passport photo. "Not my best side," she said. "I asked the man if he could just glue my perty picture at cousin Jilly's wedding—talk about a wing-ding!—but no, he had to make me look like a tree knot. Ever eat pig? At cousin Jilly's they had seven pigs roastin' away—"

"Shut mouth!" The soldier flipped through her passport pages. "Name?"

"Miss Jewel E. Jewel. Says right there I'm from Arkansas, only self-sufficient state in the Union. Suggest you pay a visit there some day, sonny, and learn yourself some manners. The 'E's for nothin', case you're askin'. Mama gave me the 'E' so I could be anything I wanted. Sometimes I'm 'Edna' and sometimes I'm 'Eliza' and sometimes I'm 'Elizabeth' but in the summertime I like 'Lizzy' because 'Lizzy'—"

I grabbed her arm. "Give it a rest, Jewel."

"My my my my my, seems like you missed your manners class, too, young man."

While the soldier inspected our passports, two other soldiers rummaged through the luggage on the bus. They shredded sacks of food and clothes and threw all the contents onto a pile outside.

They tossed four squawking chickens out the window. One of the soldiers in the bus tried to open my father's white Totes. He put Big Green up to his ear, held one of my dad's flannel shirts up to his chest, and replaced his helmet with the Indians cap.

The soldier put all these things back until he came to the Lemon Twist. He held the box at arm's length while walking slowly out the door, then placed it gently on the ground and cautiously opened it up. The other soldier holding Jewel's passport—". . .'Emma' was for the debutante ball and 'Esther' for Jilly's wedding but 'Emperor' is what I love because . . ."—stepped away and leveled his pistol at the Lemon Twist. By this time twelve soldiers had encircled it, half-certain that this big plastic lemon with a yard-long cord was some kind of bomb. Then one of the soldiers tiptoed forward and, with all the others aiming their guns at the lemon, pressed the "on" switch. Suddenly they all jumped back, startled by the yellow cord rotating on its own around the lemon. Little by little the soldiers inched back toward the circle until, confident that it was no bomb, they lowered themselves to study the counter on the lemon clicking with each revolution.

"And this," Cindy whispered to me, "is what they call a war."

Meanwhile on the bus a soldier had strapped onto his chest a very large brassiere. He sashayed down the steps carrying a J.C. Penney box, kicking aside a chicken, blowing kisses to the other hooting soldiers. He tossed a bra to each of them. Some strapped them on while others dropped them in the dirt and resumed their passport inspections.

Jewel broke from the line. "Them's mine! Them brassieres is mine and I'll be good and goddamned if you little . . . give it here! Give it here, you little goddamn black sonuvabitch!" A soldier eluded Jewel like a matador, taunting her to grab the bra before jumping aside. Cindy clapped encouragement to the soldier. "You give it here! You give it here, you goddamn sonuvabitch, or I'll kick your little black nuts up to Neptune so help me Jesus. I said *give it here*, goddamn you!"

69

He did, doubled over in laughter. Jewel scooped up all the other bras on the ground, cursing and growling, while the soldier returned to inspecting passports. He opened mine. Against my wholesome, well-fed, pasteurized face the soldier pressed his thumbnail, cracked and grimy. Then he studied Cindy's picture for a long time, a California face that knew a world this soldier could never fathom: a world of prom nights and pajama parties, of orthodontists and Frisbees, of Disneyland and yogurt and cheerleading camp.

I wanted to touch this soldier's palms and blackened fingernails. I wanted him and all the others to drop their guns for just five minutes and to step outside this war game they were playing, to enter the circle of the rotating Lemon Twist cord and to hop over it again and again like schoolgirls in a playground, giggling.

Everyone reboarded the bus, now strewn with clothes and fruit and chicken feathers. No one complained, which was sad testimony to how accustomed these people had become to chaos. They were alive and they had a place on a bus—these were triumphs enough.

The bus rolled on, passing panoramas of rice terraces and coconut groves, passing burning tires and a man on his knees with a soldier's gun to his head. At the next bus stop a dozen people somehow managed to squeeze on board, tilting the bus so much that when it rounded corners, its undercarriage sparked against the asphalt.

Our plans had changed. Cindy, between making more faces at the baby and ordering Jewel to pipe down, had decided on two things: that my father's suitcase on wheels had to go, and that this was a good time for me to be alone with him. Cindy said she could use the time to complete a site report at Jewel's school and then meet me in a week at Kandy, Sri Lanka's spiritual center. This would leave me alone with my dad, something I both wanted and dreaded. Before I had much say in the matter she was off the bus. I leaned down and saw the two of them out the back window—one white woman with egg-stained pants and a box of brassieres on her head, another white woman pulling a suitcase on wheels, both waving to me until the bus rounded a corner and began its climb into the central mountains.

And with that we were alone, my father and I. Thirty minutes on two occasions, that was the most time I could ever recall spending alone with my dad. One was our magical swim at Ocean City, the other was in 1963 on a crosstown drive to see his senile aunt in a nursing home. On that day I doubt if we talked at all, listening instead to the football game between Cleveland and Dallas on the radio three days after President Kennedy had been shot. All I remember from that ride were the barren trees along the road; all I remember of the nursing home was my father tenderly wiping away his aunt's drool; and on the drive home all I remember was the frantic report of Oswald shot by Jack Ruby, a gangster's name I instantly liked and wanted.

Near the top of the mountain my father and I stepped off the bus. I helped him down, holding out my forearm for him as if he were an old lady arriving by stagecoach. His white underwear was riding up higher than his pants.

Once on the ground he adjusted his cap and sighed. "Jimmy, it's a miracle we're alive. That driver, he's a nut. Did you see him swerve! Did you see the way he passed! Holy God, the fellow drove that bus like he'd stolen it. We're taking taxis from here on out, and I'll not hear a word about . . . Hey, where's Cindy?"

I explained, but I don't think he heard me through the roar of the receding bus and the cloud of exhaust it left behind. My dad unfurled his handkerchief and, in the few spots not already smudged with Colombo grit, wiped away the pellets of brown sweat dotting his forehead. I handed him his little backpack, which I had stuffed with a handful of clothes from that albatross of a suitcase. He didn't seem to care what I had done with that suitcase. By this point he must have concluded that his life belonged to me.

I turned him around. "Look, Dad, down there. It's the Mahaweli."

Curving through the mountains many miles below us was Sri Lanka's largest and most holy river, the Mahaweli. I pointed out to my dad that the dots of activity along its banks were people bathing or washing their clothes, and that the occasional boulder was really an elephant in for a bath. From this high vantage point we were nearly at eye level with the cumulous clouds sailing like an armada across the sky. Far off to the west, through thin smoke rising from hillside homes, we could see the holy mountain of Sri Pada. Its peak is where Sri Lankans believe the Buddha first stepped onto the earth, and it is now the destination for pilgrims from around the world. I told my father of the time Cindy and I trudged up Sri Pada through the night, sharing the steep and uneven path with sprightly eighty-year-olds without shoes or teeth. I asked my dad if he might want to try it.

"Not on your life," he said.

For a while longer he admired the river and the clouds and the mountain, his face soothed by the cooler breezes at this elevation. "OK, Jimmy," he said after a while, "where's this house you keep talking about? Let's get on with it so I can take a snooze."

I told him we still had six miles to go.

"Six miles!" He stared hard at me. "Six miles by *taxi*, I hope you mean. Because if you have some cockeyed notion of walking or, holy God, getting back on a bus, I'm afraid that—"

"Go sit down, Dad," I said, turning him around. "Go sit over there against the store and leave the transportation to me."

By chance there was a taxi parked down the road. I was relieved at its sight but uneasy at the prospect of having to negotiate a price with the driver. Cindy always did our negotiating; I would just stand off to the side with my hands crossed in front, stern and mute as a bodyguard. I needed her now.

"Say, Jim," my dad said, "isn't that a cab over there?"

"A cab? Oh, yeah, but let's just wait a bit and see if a bus comes along?"

"A bus! What, are you nuts? Run up and nab that guy before anyone else comes along."

I told him I'd see what I could do.

"See what you can do? What do you mean, you'll see what you can do! It's obvious. What you'll do is take my money and hire the fellow. Now."

I positioned my dad against an awning post and told him not to worry. He said he was very worried. I opened his Totes umbrella for him and then walked toward the taxi driver, feeling my dad's eyes boring through the back of my skull.

The driver was asleep. I shook him, then shook him harder to show that I was no pushover. *Hey, wake up,* I shouted in Sinhala. *How much to Patana?*

Without opening his eyes the driver turned aside, curling an imaginary blanket over his shoulder.

*Patana,* I shook. *How much to Patana? It's only a few kilometers, five at most. Fifty rupees, okay?*

He cracked open his eyes and folded his arms. *Five hundred,* he said, though I wasn't sure I heard right through his thick mustache drooping over his mouth. *Five hundred,* he repeated, then turned back into sleep.

I called him a thief, a negotiating tactic I'd seen others use.

He suddenly sat up, very awake. *A thief? You call me a thief? Then you come pay the thief seven hundred rupees to Patana.*

*Listen,* I chuckled, now trying the friendly tactic, *I said you aren't a thief. You're a good man. And so is my father. Do you see him over there, the old man with the umbrella? He is ill and we must be good to our fathers. One hundred rupees, okay?*

*He is sick? Then eight hundred rupees. This is no ambulance service.*

I called him a thief and he raised the price two hundred rupees.

*To Patana,* he said, his hands chopping the air for emphasis, *it is hilly and dangerous. Who gets my car out if it is stuck in the mud? If I am killed sliding down the mountain, who supports my two blind children—not one, two!*

*Look at my father. If he dies, do you want his blood on your hands? And all for a little money! Two hundred rupees, final.*

*Two blind children. One useless wife.*

*I sacrifice two years of my life for your country and the least you can do is—*

*Who can afford gas these days? This war kills a part of us all every day.*

*Have a heart. Three hundred rupees, final.*

He turned aside and closed his eyes. *One thousand and not one rupee less,* he said, then began to snore.

I was no negotiating slouch. I knew the game: start to walk away and he will call me back, begging to drive us to Patana for fifty rupees. I walked, but after ten yards there was no call. I slowed down. I turned an ear, turned a face. In disbelief I turned a whole body: no call. Through the rear window of the taxi I saw the crown of his head rising and falling with the rhythms of his sleep. What should I do? I took one step back to the cab and then stopped, realizing that this was a matter of pride. No one, I ranted to myself, is going to *toy with my money!* With those words came the troubling thought that I had become my father, bashing the Nebraska Coke machine, while my dad, pressing his palm against the awning column to form an imprint on his skin, had become little me in the back seat of the Delta 88.

I avoided this thought as best I could and walked over to my father. "Not a chance, Dad," I said, shaking my head. "He's not going our way."

He lowered his Totes to machine-gun position and stared at me in disbelief. "What do you mean, not going our way? Does he have so much business that he can be choosy? If it's a question of money, Jimmy, I'll—"

"No, no, no, no, no," I chuckled. "That's the least of my worries, Dad."

74

Before he could say anything more, a bus approached. It was ludicrously crowded, and at its sight I could feel my dad's irritation prick into me.

"Holy God, Jimmy, we're gonna have to wait for the next one."

I nudged the toe of one sandal into the heel of the other. "There is no next one, Dad."

"You can't be serious."

"I'm afraid it's either this one or we walk."

He looked over at the sleeping taxi. "Can't you offer that fella—" but before he could finish his sentence I had begun to push him into the block of flesh on the bus, my arms around him, my chest pressing him deeper into some crevice. The bus started to move with my feet still on the ground. Some kind of peristaltic action swallowed my father into the bus while I, running, reached for two of the dozen outstretched arms. They lifted me, my feet dangling in midair until the tip of my toe found the edge of a step. My body angled outwards like a water skier, the two arms of strangers holding me firm. From my position on these mountain roads I could look straight down cliff sides, and though after two years I had become accustomed to treacherous bus rides, it was clear to me then that I could easily fall off and die. That would leave my father to sort out his worst nightmare: completely alone and adrift in the middle of Sri Lanka.

I managed to slither inside the bus. I found room to stand when a woman rose onto her toes for a moment, creating space beneath her heel that I filled. She scowled up at me, the two gold studs flaring on the wings of her nose. At the next stop nobody got off and eight got on, including a couple of merchants selling newspapers and *wadee*s, a fried hockey puck made of lentils. The *wadee* man's face looked like a giant *wadee* itself, dark and pitted and shiny with grease. He screamed "Wadee-wadee-wadee-wadee-wadee" into my ear and balanced his basket on my shoulder.

*I'll take five,* I told him.

"Wadee-wadee-wadee?"

*Yeah, I'll take five.*

He smiled, flashing his jagged and stained teeth up at me. He spiraled a sheet of yesterday's newspaper into a cone, tossed in five *wadee*s and then, as an afterthought, threw in two more. Just then I felt an insistent tap on my shoulder.

"I need some air, Jimmy. I can't breathe."

I turned and saw my father, white and unsteady. "We're almost there, Dad. Hang on just a bit more." I pitied him. I wanted to press an eject button to catapult him onto the plains of Kansas. I wanted to slit open my own lungs so he could suck on young air. "Five more minutes at most. I promise."

"I need some space, Jimmy. Quick."

But there was no space to be had—not on this bus, not in Sri Lanka. In a place like this the space of America seemed even vaster: vast backyards, vast aisles in supermarkets, vast road lanes, vast Nebraska. That kind of public space influences the American notion of private space, too. *My* bedroom, *my* journal, *my* wallet—stay out of them, and stay out of my salary and out of my secrets. American space is my birthright.

Congestion is the Sri Lankan birthright. In the world's second most densely populated country, the congestion is public (this bus, those bikes and cows and beggars sharing the road) and private (What is your salary? Why have you no children? What is that pimple doing on your forehead?). It makes sense that Buddhism should thrive in such a dense society. Its central belief, that individuality is an illusion, is apparent every second of the day to a people crammed into buses and marketplaces. With very little public space or solitude, Sri Lankans rely on Buddhist meditation to find a pocket of internal peace. Not so in America, where Buddhism will remain on the fringes as long as there is the Grand Canyon, and Delta 88s, and 167 golf courses in the Phoenix area alone.

Soon our crammed bus stopped and we elbowed our way outside. My dad muttered "Holy God" a few times and straightened out his baseball cap. The bus crawled away beneath its heavy load, its cloud of exhaust enshrouding us. Once the cloud lifted, though, we stood in the center of a new land. Surrounding us and rolling out to the horizon were light-green bushes of tea, all pruned waist-high for easy picking. Stooping throughout the bushes were the tea pickers, all women, dressed in brightly colored saris and carrying baskets attached by rope to their foreheads. That's all there was. No buses, no soldiers, no beggars, no noise, no sweat—just tea, green and fragrant and endless tea.

"Isn't it gorgeous, Dad?"

"Huh?"

"I said it's spectacular, don't you think?"

"I'm exhausted, and that's that."

A few feet away stood two rows of eucalyptus trees flanking a stream. I pointed to the rutted dirt road next to the trees winding along the mountainside. "We have to walk a little bit now, Dad. Not too far. Here, you want a wadee?"

He sneered at the greasy puck and then hoisted his pack over his shoulder as if it were a cross. "How far is not too far?"

"The walk? Oh, not so far. And we'll just take our time and enjoy all this beautiful—"

"I'm not interested in beauty right now, Jim. I'm tired. And it seems like we've been traveling for a year."

"Well, you know what they say about the journey itself being the destination."

"Never heard of it." He turned away from me and looked down the dirt road. "My destination better be a bed, that's all I can say. I'm exhausted."

"Hang in there, Dad. Not much further. Or is it 'farther'? I could never get those two straight."

77

"Spare me the grammar and get me a bed." He stopped and wobbled. "I'm feeling a bit faint, too."

Seeing him like this made we wonder what I would do if my dad collapsed on me then, right there on that hillside silent with tea. The moon seemed closer to me than the nearest hospital. How slim were the odds that any of these tea pickers knew CPR, and if they did, what would my dad think if, resuscitated, he stared square into a black and toothless mouth rimmed with the same red betel juice dribbling down his own throat?

"Dad, let me carry your pack for you."

He looked up at the eucalyptus trees and out to the horizon of tea, then over to the path that wound deeper and deeper into the mountains.

"I'd appreciate that, Jimmy," he said, and slid his backpack down his arm and handed it to me.

6

The path to Vijay's house was overrun with lemon grass as tall as
our eyes. My father and I thrashed through it, unable to see two
feet ahead of us until we reached a clearing. There we saw a Tamil
family frozen at the impossible sight of us, two tall white hairy
blue-eyed men. All of them were crammed into two railroad boxcars
called "line houses." The British had installed them a century ago to
shelter the thousands of southern Indians imported to pick tea.
Today, the Sinhalese government did little to improve their situation. Jobs, roads, schools, houses, medicine—the Tamil tea picker
living on the sides of these steep hills was sure to get nothing,
especially during this heightened stage of civil war. They were the
shadow people of Sri Lanka, the poorest and the least educated,
the most isolated and the most ridiculed. Even the civil war wasn't
interested in these ragged hills. In this and many ways these Tamils
regarded themselves as invisible to the outside world, so that whenever Cindy and I would greet them with *wanacome* (the Tamil version
of *ayubowan*), they'd be astonished that we had noticed them at all.
I ached at their neglect, and I knew how much a greeting from my
dad would mean to them, bearing the multiple status of old and
white and male and American—plus he was a guest.

"Just try it, Dad. It's easy: 'Wanacome.'"

"No, no. Don't start in with the language lessons now."

"Just pretend you're a barber back in Cleveland asking for a comb. 'Hey, you *want a comb?'* Get it? Want a comb, wanacome. Give it a try."

"Listen, Jimmy. All I want to try now is a bed. I'm exhausted."

The entire family stood mesmerized as we walked by. Out of respect for us they stayed inside their boxcars, their blue-black faces filling the windows and the open door. The only one left outside was a deformed girl sitting on the ground, rocking herself in the shadow of a tree. Suddenly a little boy sprinted out from the house toward us, offering a mango, until his father snatched him up in midair and spanked him all the way back inside.

From across the valley came the noon broadcast of the Muslim call to prayer. My dad, walking backwards to keep an eye on the Tamil family, paid no attention to the music of the prayer. Instead he stepped square into a mound of cow dung and, until I redirected him, was nearly skewered on the horn of a water buffalo. A mongrel dog bared its fangs at him. A woman who was scraping up the dung to use as fuel threw a coconut shell at the dog, then bowed to my father and slid away into the tall lemon grass. My dad tipped his Indians cap to her, but the grass had already swallowed her up.

We saw Vijay's five sisters before they saw us. They were sitting toboggan-style on their front porch, each searching for ticks in the other's hair. My dad knew what they were up to.

"Say, Jim," he said, tightening his baseball cap, "aren't those hair bugs able to jump?"

"Yeah, but just short distances."

"That's the only distance I care about right now. From Delaware to Louisiana, I don't care, but head to head, that's suddenly my business."

When we entered their yard all five girls darted inside. Vijay's mother then shuffled out to greet us, wiping her hands on the skirt of her sari. Her five daughters followed closely behind, their eyes on the ground. A couple of hens squawked out of the way and ran into the house. I thought I heard a goat screeching inside one of the two outhouses.

Vijay emerged from indoors, smiling and enthusiastic, his arms spread wide. "Jim and Mr. Jim's father! Oh, this is the greatest of honors to have you visit my house."

We embraced. I could see up close that his twenty-two-year-old face, black and hairless, was already wrinkled from the burden of being the eldest son in a family without a father. His family managed to live on his meager salary as a teacher, earned from three months teaching Sinhala to Peace Corps volunteers, then nine months teaching every subject to tea plantation children. Though talented and bright, Vijay could reach no higher position in this country that based promotions more on race than on merit.

He introduced us to his family. They were all on their knees, bent at the waist, hands together in prayer. To them we were gods—not just demigods, but manifestations of real gods. As Vijay went down the line introducing his sisters to us, I instructed my dad to touch their heads lightly with his fingertips. He whispered to me that he would do no such thing.

"Dad, please. It's their custom, and if you don't they'll see it as an insult."

"Yeah, well, I'm in no hurry to make friends with those hair critters. Besides, whatever happened to a handshake?"

His uneasiness was a revelation to me. The slippery art of the introduction, which he had mastered as a Cleveland judge, now confounded him here in Sri Lanka. For years he had been the smooth one, and when I accompanied him to political rallies or funerals (especially funerals; the Irish can't get enough of those funerals), he would meet new people with grace and ease. He remembered names. He knew how to touch elbows, how to tilt at the waist, how to lilt his voice. "Clair! Clair Kennedy!" he'd say, his two hands gloving her one. "My oh my, Clair, your brother and me went back to the days at Cathedral Latin when . . ." Eventually he'd get around to introducing me, panicked and blinking, overwhelmed as if Clair were delivering a baby on the spot. To Clair, whose name I had forgotten the moment I heard it, I would extend my limp, clammy hand, and look away.

Here on this hillside of tea, then, I rather liked my dad's distress. I wanted him to feel like slithering into the lemon grass.

Eventually, after more nudging from me, my dad touched the daughters' heads as if each were a hot stove. When he stood before the mother, she looked up into his eyes and, pressing her hands together beneath her chin, said, "Wanacome." My dad's hands came halfway together. His lips moved into some vague shape of "wanacome," though it could just have likely been "want a hairbrush."

Vijay led us indoors, kicking a chicken out of his way. My father and I ducked our heads beneath the entrance and then stood in the four-room house, its walls and floor made of mud, its roof of asbestos sheeting. I told my dad that this asbestos roof was cheap and common in Sri Lanka, courtesy of American or West German companies that could no longer dump their carcinogenic products on their own people. He said "ah-hah" as if his mind were elsewhere.

It was on the house. He peeked his head into the dark rooms to scout the horrors awaiting him here, like whether his bed for the night would be made from a hollowed-out cow. All seemed fine for the moment. Then he saw a table of food covered with newspapers dotted with hundreds of flies. While backing away in disgust, he bumped his head into a bizarre decoration hanging from the ceiling. It was Vijay's art, an IV tube that he had twisted and knotted into the image of a fish. It too was black with flies, all rising when my father knocked the fish with his head. For a few seconds the flies buzzed madly around my dad's head like electrons, then settled back down on the fish.

"Holy God," he growled, swatting the air. "How did I end up in this stockyard at my age?"

Vijay led us into the kitchen to meet his grandmother. We peered in from the doorway, adjusting our eyes to the dimness and the smoke. In the far corner, lit by a small fire, squatted the grainy shape of an old woman. She was cutting vegetables in the Sri Lankan way: anchoring the knife on the ground between her splayed toes, blade side up, and swiftly moving the onion across the blade with her hands.

"Now that's a new one," my dad whispered to me. "Never thought you could use a knife like that, turned upside-down. Here I go a whole lifetime thinking there's only one way to cut an onion. Jimmy, remind me to tell your mother about this one."

The grandmother's toes made fresh imprints in the layer of cow dung spread thinly across the mud floor. She glanced up at us, the gold hoop in her nostril glinting in the firelight. My dad tipped his Indians cap to her. She stared at him, stared a little longer and a little more deeply, then turned her shoulder into the corner of the room and spat red betel juice into a tin can. She hid her mouth behind a flap of sari and resumed cutting.

I looked at her and my father. What was happening here in the doorway, between light and dark, between civilizations, between centuries? Though of the same age, what could this woman be to my dad: more mushroom than woman? More dung and darkness than a lady with wit and fire? In that moment when their eyes met, what secret language did they exchange?

"I have to sit," my dad said. A hen ran out from beneath the grandmother's sari, squawking. "I have to sit *now*. Better yet, can you find me a bed?"

Vijay, worried about his hospitality, asked if he could get my dad some water or tea. "Or food. Perhaps the sir needs some rice or wadees or—"

"Sleep. All I need is a little catnap, Vijoo."

83

"Dad, it's 'Vijay.'"

"Vijay, Vooji—whatever. All I know is that I've been put through the wringer all day, so just point me to the nearest bed and clear the way."

En route to the bedroom my dad once again hit his head against the plastic fish, releasing the flies. Swatting and cursing he bumped into the table of food, jarring all those flies resting on the newspaper into orbit around his head. "Jesus, Mary, and Joseph!" he cursed, beating the air. "May God in heaven give me strength."

I closed the bedroom door behind him. Vijay motioned me over to the front window, where we stood watching his little sisters outside mimicking my dad, wildly swatting imaginary flies. They laughed so hard that they all fell down. "I'm sorry, Jim," Vijay said, "if we disrespect your . . . your . . ." But he too started to giggle, then to laugh hysterically, and so did I, though I think my laughter came more from the pleasure of seeing these people full of joy in a time when joy was scarce.

Vijay and I sat and talked. While catching up on our lives we let our fingers entwine around each other's in the custom of good Sri Lankan friends—strictly male to male, that is, or female to female. Eventually our discussion led to Ranji.

"I have seen her, Jim," Vijay whispered. "For the last couple of weeks, every day we meet while her father is cutting rice."

"Does he know? The father?"

"I'm sure he does but she doesn't care." For a year Vijay had been in love with a woman whose father had already chosen her mate. Vijay, too, had an arranged partner, though as the eldest son he first had to wait until all five of his sisters were married. If Vijay broke all the rules and did marry Ranji, both families would banish them, a consequence too grave in this small, religious society. He tightened his fingers around mine. "I must be with her, Jim.

I must be with her or I die. I know it is not right for her, for my sisters, for our . . ."

One of Vijay's sisters entered the room, kneeling at his feet for permission to leave the house. After he lightly touched her head, she backed out of the room without raising her eyes, her front always facing us.

"For that sister, for the others, I must wait," Vijay said. "But how many more years must I wait for my freedom? Ten? Fifteen? And then my wife is *chosen* for me. Do you see how I am trapped, Jim? Do you see how in my world Ranji is an impossibility but Ranji is all that I want?"

Another sister, barefoot and eyes down, drifted in with a tray of tea and *wadees*. Flies dotted her arms like freckles, and as she turned to leave, the scent of kitchen smoke and *wadee* grease rose off her sari.

"You in America have it right," Vijay said between sips of tea. "You are free to do what *you* want, not what your mother or your culture tells you to do. It is primitive, this system. Imagine: You meet Cindy and you love Cindy and then you *can't* marry her because your parents have a strange woman chosen for you, a woman you've *never* seen before. This is barbaric. Why does God put love inside of us if not to be used? Is it only for suffering that God makes me love Ranji and she love me?"

"But, Vijay, look how love fails in America." I explained what I had often told Sri Lankans, that America is not the love paradise Vijay may think it is, that it is a land of disillusionment and divorce and families spread thousands of miles apart. "Over here these arranged marriages seem to work. The partners stay together and love usually grows between them."

"It is a business arrangement, Jim. It gives me a business partner, not Ranji, the woman I love. It places business above love, and I cannot live that way. This is torture for me. This is not life for me."

85

The highest suicide rate in Asia belongs to Sri Lanka, almost all because of this situation Vijay was in. These young, trapped lovers most often swallowed DDT, the pesticide banned in America but sold by American companies to Sri Lankan farmers.

"So, Jim, I must ask you again to help me get to America. You see that I have no future here. Find me a university, a job, any job. I will work in your McDonalds. I'll do anything."

"You know I'll never do that, Vijay." He knew my stance on the immigration topic: I wouldn't contribute to the "brain drain" of Sri Lanka's brightest, even though I was badgered daily by desperate Sri Lankans and offered plenty of bribes. Personally, I wanted Vijay alongside me in America, hiking in Yosemite and shelling peanuts at a baseball game. But to do so would dishonor the Peace Corps and wound his sisters, his students, and his Tamil community at a time when they most needed him. I was there to celebrate and reinforce his culture, not to chip it away. "I'm doing you a favor by doing nothing, Vijay."

"I know, I know. And I respect you and I know I belong here, with my people. But look at it this way: Who's going to introduce wadees to America if I don't come over? And who's going to teach your father how to make fish out of IV tubes?"

My father! I suddenly remembered that I had a father in the next room. I rose to check on him, concerned that the flies might have nibbled through to his intestines while he slept. When I peered into his room, however, I saw that my dad had solved the fly problem for the Third World napper. He had covered himself from head to toe with newspapers like the food on the table.

"Vijay," I whispered, "come here and see an American judge in all his glory. Call your sisters, too."

Together the seven of us watched from the door, pinching our noses to keep from laughing at this body shrouded in newspaper. The paper crackled with the rising and falling of his breath. Gradually, his hand slid down from his stomach and dangled limp near the floor, his rosary still encircling his wrist. A couple of flies landed on his thumb.

"Holy God," he moaned, flicking his fingers. He returned his hand to his chest and murmured some prayers in time with the clicking of his rosary.

We all snickered. But at this moment, seeing my dad on a hard wooden bed, his body wrapped in paper like meat from a butcher's, I couldn't help but love the old guy. In such weak, exposed moments I loved him the most. My pinched snicker nearly made the short leap to tears, and all I wanted to do was to toss aside the newspaper and fan my father like a pharaoh, all day and all night.

We returned to our chairs and soon heard my dad stirring. The newspaper rustled, the wood slats creaked, my dad pleaded to God, and soon he was standing before Vijay and me with his pants twisted to one side and his hair tousled high and wild. He wagged a finger at both of us.

"Think I didn't hear you in there, laughing at your old man like that?" His serious expression gave way to a laugh. "I wish I could've seen it myself, me and a bedsheet made of the day's news. If you ask me it's a pretty clever fly repellent. Now, Jimmy, don't you be babbling about this back home or Malone, he'll get wind of it and it's yammer yammer yammer up and down the courthouse halls. I can hear that jackass now."

I was glad he was in a good mood because we were about to eat, a cultural experience that was sure to set him back. My dad and I sat down at the table, the cane on the seat of our chairs creaking beneath our weight. I didn't trust the frayed cane, so I sat on the wooden edge and left fate to deal with my dad.

No one ate with us. Vijay's mother and sisters would eat later in the kitchen squatting on inch-high benches; Vijay would follow us at the table. But for now the entire family had the single-minded duty of serving us. They brought in plates of curried vegetables in coconut milk, saffron rice with cashews and raisins, fish, fruit, avocados, and tea, all laid on a new tablecloth which I'm sure Vijay's mother had sewn just for our arrival. Once our plates were full the entire family stood against the walls waiting for our next need.

My dad elbowed me. "Where are the forks?"

"Attached to your wrists."

"Wrists? What's that supposed to mean?"

"You use your fingers, Dad. Just pretend you're eating a hamburger or pizza. You wouldn't want a fork for a burger, would you?"

He looked at his plate. "This here is no juicy burger, believe you me. Malone, I remember him telling me all about this. Told me to bring my own fork wherever I went. 'Bring a dozen, John,' he said, 'or else you'll come home with food stuck under your nails for months.'" He lowered his eyes to the plate. "I just hope there's nothing moving in there. Malone told me all kinds of stories about microbes that turn big as eels once they get inside the human belly."

I wanted to slap him—nothing hard, just a light friendly smack or two. I just couldn't understand how he could be so afraid of food. Here was the judge who stared down all those criminals in his Cleveland courtroom, those hatchet murderers eager to rip off his head. Then he'd go to lunch (every day a tuna sandwich from Wally the blind vendor) before returning to an afternoon docket of rapists and wife-bashers. All these thugs cowered before him, and yet now he trembled in front of a plate of rice.

"Take the plunge, Dad. It's time for all good men to be courageous. Just gather the food at the tips of your fingers, like this, and—"

"Hold it, hold it, hold it," he said, raising his hand. "I believe you're forgetting something here, Jimmy."

"What?"

"Does the word 'grace' ring a bell around here, as in 'grace before meals'?" He cleared his throat, straightened his back, and adjusted his butt on the creaking cane. He shut his eyes tight. "Let us begin. Dear Jesus, we are gathered here before you . . ."

This worried me. I was hungry, I was salivating, and this guy's long-winded grace was going to keep all this exquisite food out of my mouth. He had done this before. I remembered all those Thanksgivings when the steam rising off the sliced turkey would disappear while my father prayed on and on and on.

"The good Lord has brought me safely from another continent to sit at this Sri Lankan table with my Jimmy. Our Lord has gathered us to give him thanks, and to thank Voojoo and his family for this wonderful food"—his eyes opened, as if hoping to find corn-on-the-cob and steak and a pitcher of Ohio spring water, then shut them tight—"food which the good Lord in all His mystery has seen fit to provide for us. In addition, let us pray . . ."

He was just warming up. It would be a while before he would dismount from this horse—so familiar, so satisfying, so free of eels. But it was torturing me, and I thought of screaming a samurai scream and burying my mouth in the mountain of food on my plate. I glanced everywhere else to get my mind off the food, first up to see the house cat leaning down from the space between the roof and wall, then over to see Vijay and his sisters biting their lips not to laugh.

"Let us pray with all our fervent hearts for the poor people up here in the mountains of Sri Lanka who have little money and little houses full of chickens and flies and hard wood beds and yet who provide us with food which the Lord in all His goodness . . ."

The cat on the wall pawed downward. My stomach growled. The cane beneath my dad's butt creaked. My stomach growled.

"Let us never forget what the Lord taught us about the least of thy brethren being the first in the Kingdom"—he sagged lower into the chair, and the cat leaned farther—"to stand alongside God who in all His majesty has made all things possible. Let us never forget"—lower, a gentle oozing, a popping of threads—"that Christ Jesus saw fit to—"

*TWANG!* The cane gave way and my dad fell through and the cat jumped into a bowl of fish. Everybody froze. In that frozen moment I marveled that the stuff of bad slapstick could happen in real life. And in that moment I thought: My kingdom for a camera. Then the scene unfroze and the cat leaped into a corner, leaving curried paw prints on the new tablecloth. My father could see those prints quite well because his head had dropped to the level of the table. He wasn't laughing. No one in that room was, least of all Vijay's mother, who was so mortified that she shrunk into the corner with the cat. But from another room there was a high-pitched whoop, and there inside the doorway to the smoky kitchen squatted the grandmother on her haunches, rocking, laughing herself to tears, pointing at my father with her crooked brown finger.

My dad squirmed. "Get me out of here, Jimmy."

I tried to pry him out of the chair but all that lifted was the entire apparatus, twanged chair and white rump now united like a mythological creature. Vijay's mother shrunk farther into the corner, wringing her hands on the skirt of her sari.

"Oh God, Dad," I said, "you look ridiculous. Wait'll I tell Mom about this one. And Malone."

"Don't you dare. Don't you dare whisper one word to Malone or I'm done for sure. Now get me out."

"Sorry, can't. You're stuck in this chair for life, so may as well get used to it. Hey, look at the bright side: You'll never have to stand on a Sri Lankan bus again."

Word was already spreading throughout the tea estate of what had just happened. A few neighbors leaned through the open window, and I could see behind them a dozen more running up from the road. This was an event, maybe the event of their lifetimes, and no one was going to miss the chance to be an eyewitness. By now Vijay's mother was in hiding; the grandmother was out in the open, howling in laughter; and I was suggesting to Vijay that he ought to charge admission.

"Like the baboon lady at a carnival side-show," I said, then turned to my dad as he was inching his way out of the chair. "Not so fast, Dad. We've decided to wrap a cobra around your neck and have you juggle swords, just to make a few bucks. So settle back on down and be a sport, okay?"

"It's not funny, Jimmy. And it's starting to hurt."

We did free him, eventually, and all the eyewitnesses went home to spread the gospel of the Cane Chair Plunge. It wouldn't take long for this story to reach the farthest edges of Sri Lanka.

We still had to eat. Vijay brought in a new chair for my dad, this one reinforced with enough two-by-fours to support an elephant. Then I taught him how to eat: mash together some of the curries and rice into a ball, twirl it tight, move it up to the tip of the fingers, keep your elbow high, then pop it like a marble with your thumb into your mouth. "See, Dad," I demonstrated. "It's neat and clean."

But nothing he did was neat or clean. Rice kernels fell on his lap and on the floor, bouncing into corners for the chickens to fight over. Very little ended up in his mouth.

"Keep your elbow up higher, Dad, and pack the food tighter."

He tried again. This time he flicked the food with his index finger, not his thumb, sending a missile of rice across the room. The chickens were upon it in seconds. The grandmother was watching all of this from the kitchen entrance, shaking her head.

"Use your thumb, Dad, your thumb. Not your pinky, your *thumb!*"

Finally, after more misfires that shot rice up to the ceiling, he got it: The ball of rice landed in his mouth, and from down on her haunches the grandmother applauded.

"Oh yes!" my dad gloated. "Looks like this old dog can still learn a few tricks."

But on his own without my guiding hand he never really got it. He sprayed rice on the floor and in his lap and in my hair, and when the curry juices started dribbling down his chin, I thought, "My father, a baby in a high chair." Yet I was worried about this baby who hadn't eaten much since he arrived. I mashed a solid ball of food from my plate and held it up to his mouth.

"C'mon, Dad. You have to eat."

He pushed my hand away. "I'll be fine, Jimmy. I'm sure I'll be fine."

After dinner my dad and I petted the cow and talked baseball, and when it was time for him to prepare for bed, I showed him to the outhouse.

There were two of them, and it was very important to keep them straight. The smaller one was for the women of the house, but it also doubled as a cage for the goat, though no one ever explained why the goat had to be "outhoused" at night. Next to it stood the men's room. Unlike the open-pit toilet in the women's, ours had a porcelain, water-sealed basin cemented into the ground straddled by a pair of large footprints. "This toilet comes from India," Vijay boasted. "The first on the plantation." In the corner stood a fifty-five-gallon drum containing all the water for all the ablutions. I told my dad to scoop out a handful to brush his teeth.

"*That* water?" he said. "In *my* mouth? You've got to be kidding."

"Just swish it around a little and don't drink it. Trust me. You'll be fine."

He had that look of someone who's not sure if he's the butt of a practical joke. I had seen it before in five-year-old Jackie Carlin, the neighborhood sucker, when he inspected an Oreo cookie from us older boys. Jackie would sniff and squish the Oreo, half-certain that we had laced the white inner cream with dish soap and cat food. He was right, but he usually shrugged and ate it anyway.

"If I do any swishing," my dad said, "I'll be on the pot all night. Malone warned me about this. 'John, better to put a loaded gun to your head than drink a spot of that gutter water.'" In the neighboring outhouse the goat was getting restless, thumping his legs against the wall. "I'll bet that damn goat is trying to tell me a thing or two."

"Dad, I promise that you won't get sick. I've been swishing this stuff for two years now and," I lied, "I've never been sick."

"Malone wouldn't lie. That goat wouldn't lie. You, I'm not so sure about."

Eventually he dampened his toothbrush with a few sprinkles of water, brushed, then spat it all out a dozen times. "Oh good God in heaven," he sighed wearily, "bless my poor belly tonight."

With his teeth cleaned we turned to the toilet. At the mention of it he looked very old and very sad—sad that the human body couldn't hold its own waste for a month, sad that there wasn't a commode on which to sit for an hour and read the sports page. He moaned and said, "Just show me what to do and leave me a little privacy."

"Okay. The trick is to put both feet on the prints, like this, and then squat all the way down like a grasshopper, or like a catcher."

"Yogi Berra I'm not, or that cricket fella—Timony? Bimony? Look, Jim, I'm seventy-four years old and if I get down like that you'll need a crane to hoist me back up."

"You'll get the hang of it in no time. Just remember to line yourself up over the hole in the ground or you'll have a mess on your hands."

He stared down at the toilet. "Where does it all go? Are there pipes down there? Filtration plants?"

"Filtration plants! Are you putting me on?" I laughed at the idea of anything so organized, clean, modern, and expensive in Sri Lanka. Whenever I told Sri Lankans about the "modern advancements" in America—ATM machines, cable TV, funeral homes, poodles groomed to look like shrubbery—they thought I must be inventing it all. "I don't know, Dad. I guess it just goes right into the ground beneath us."

"Raw sewage straight into the soil? Is that what you're telling me?"

"Well, yeah, but it's not as gross as you make it sound. I guess it turns to manure down there, and, you know, nourishes the earth."

"*Nourishes!* Hey, I don't care if it turns to Lemon Pledge down there, it still is raw sewage going right into the ground and into rivers and eventually"—he looked at the fifty-five-gallon drum—"into the water I just used to brush my teeth."

While he spat out every atom of moisture from his mouth, I told him that some things were best left unexamined. "Now do your business and give a holler if you need me."

He held my forearm. "One more stupid question before you abandon your poor father. Toilet paper. Where do they stash it?"

I noticed on the far wall a spider the size of a hand crawling toward my dad's towel on the door. It was harmless, I knew, but I thought it best to shoo it away without my dad noticing. From the other outhouse we heard the frantic shriek and kick of the goat.

"There isn't any toilet paper, Dad," I said. "You'll just have to do what they do in Sri Lanka: Use your left hand."

He stared at me without blinking. "Run that by me again."

I explained the process to him: pour water with a cup from behind with the right hand, splatter and wipe from underneath with the left hand. But from his glazed look I think he was doing less listening to me and more fantasizing about two-ply Charmin.

"Let me see if I have this straight: You're talking about the human hand, right?" He held out his doomed left hand like it was on death row. "This hand has been good to me for seventy-four undefiled years now. This hand has held watermelons and babies. This hand has spanked you—but maybe not enough." The goat was beginning to go berserk in the outhouse next door. "I told you that goat was warning me to run away, didn't I?"

"Actually, Dad, once you get the hang of this toilet business, you'll see how perfectly it works."

"Oh, but of course."

"Really, it's a wonder to me we don't do it this way in America."

"Me too! Me too!" He raised his left hand in front of my face. "From here on out it's the hand or nothing for your mother and me. If guests don't like it, too bad. Malone might squawk but he'll come around."

"Seriously, Dad, it's even more sanitary than the American way."

"You're preaching to the converted, son."

"Why we save that stuff on paper I'll never know. All you do here is splash a little water and voilà."

"Voilà indeed!"

"Then just wash your hands real good with the soap over there."

"Awwww, is that really necessary?"

"Don't get sassy on me now. Believe me, you'll see how sanitary and effective this whole business really is. I'm serious."

"Me too. After all, what could be more sanitary than wiping your bum with your hand? Voilà, I say."

The spider was off the wall and onto his towel. I moved toward it, wondering how I was going to get rid of it without panicking my dad.

"Don't bother," he said.

I gave him an innocent look. "Don't bother about what?"

"That bad boy spider is the least of my worries. Right now I'd trade a thousand black widows for one American Standard toilet. So just leave it alone, and leave me alone."

Later that night my father and I slept in the same room on twin beds, our only cushion a thin grass mat over the wood planks. On the table between us Vijay had dimmed the oil lamp down to a point. He reminded us to avoid the left outhouse during the night—"The goat is sure to kick you"—and then tugged on my toes and wished us goodnight. I asked him where he was sleeping.

"In the next room, on the floor. I'm used to it."

"Oh, don't be a martyr. Come sleep here and I'll sleep with my dad."

"No, no, no. I like to be close to the earth. I'm not as soft as you Americans."

My dad turned on his side. "Soft? Is this your idea of soft? Holy God, I feel like I'm sleeping on nails."

Vijay closed the door on the way out. For a long time I stared at the point of light in the oil lamp, thinking too much. My dad never really fell asleep, moaning "Holy God!" every few minutes above the creek of his bed's wood planks. Each "Holy God" pricked me in the organ that holds Catholic guilt in a child, especially when he sat up on the side of the bed, digging his knuckles into his eye sockets. "Holy Mother of God, pray for me."

He had to pee. Because of his prostate, my dad now had to rise and journey through his own nightmare: flies on plastic fish, hens, bodies sleeping on the floor, a goat, a howling grandmother. The faint light of the lantern played across his gray and sunken face. My impulse while lying there was to rise with him, to escort him through the mine fields and to wait like a sentry beside the outhouse.

But vying with that impulse was another, wiser one: Let him be. Let him face the demons of the night on his own at the one time in his life when he can no longer avoid them. Just let him be.

He made it out of the room, then whacked his head and kicked someone and moaned "Oh good God in heaven" into the night. Then it was silent. He had made it outside, but when I didn't hear a door open I knew he must be standing before the two outhouses, gnawing his lower lip, trying to remember. I imagined him murmuring "eeny-meeny-miny-mo" and cutting deals with God. Suddenly, I heard one of the doors open, a goat screech and thump, a door slam, and an old man moan, "Oh Jesus, Mary, and Joseph."

I turned onto my stomach and buried my face into my arms. Now what was he enduring? I recalled the true story of a Peace Corps volunteer whose nighttime visit to an outhouse ended when a monitor lizard, having hidden in the toilet hole, sprung up to bite the very ample target of her very white ass. At this thought I reached over to my dad's rosary on his bed, and on each of the fifty beads I prayed, "God, no lizards tonight, Amen. God, no lizards tonight, Amen. God, no lizards . . ."

Some time later he shuffled back to our bedroom. His pajama bottoms were twisted to the side and spattered wet but, alleluia, free of lizard marks. He sat down on the edge of the bed without sighing. He lay down on the wood planks without sighing. He turned his back on me without sighing.

There were no sighs left in this broken old man.

It was unlikely that my father would fall asleep that night, but if he did I feared that his dreams would feature me, the slave driver in the bowels of a Viking ship. My dad would be a galley slave, begrimed and scarred, sitting on a bench as hard as his bed. While straining to pull the massive oar he would turn to his slave mates, Kirk Douglas and the goat, and conspire, "Tonight. Tonight, ay matees, let's rip that bastard Jimmy's throat clean out!"

And so once again I prayed: Dear God, let this father of mine have the sweetest of dreams tonight. Let goats lick his toes. Let soldiers throw him Frisbees in the glittering ocean. Let his left hand be as sanitized and sparkling as a burnished silver fork. And let a half-dressed Betty Grable feed him grapes near a shaded river.

He woke up with the slightest of smiles and the slightest skip in his step.

Maybe the smile was from Betty. But more likely that smile reflected the start of a shift within my dad during the night. The flies, the left hand, the hard bed, the journey to the outhouse—to him these were horrors, and yet by being forced to face them all alone, maybe he was coming to realize that the horrors he'd been guarding against all this time were really thin as masks. Hey, he *could* do this Sri Lankan thing after all—and live! Perhaps a little unsanitary, perhaps a bit uncomfortable, but nothing lethal and nothing more frightening than one's own shame. I'd like to think that the skip in his step that morning came from his having started to shed the weight of all the artillery he'd been lugging around to fight these phantom fears. Now he could skip, and now he could float. He could let go of that rope tying him back to his Cleveland condominium and just float in this new land with hard beds (you get used to them) and outhouses (fresh air) and new toilet customs (damn if that left hand business *doesn't* work!).

Over the next few days, bit by bit, I saw my father meet Sri Lanka. He mastered the art of finger eating and even asked for seconds. He studied the grandmother cleaning rice in the kitchen, at first standing over her blocking the doorway, later on his own haunches next to her by the fire, helping her pick out stones. He named the goat "Malone" and took it for long walks on a rope through the tea bushes. He asked the tea plantation manager how tea is dried, asked Vijay what it was like to grow up surrounded by tea, and, to my surprise, asked me if I missed America.

One day at my father's request we walked three miles down a steep embankment to visit Vijay's school. Since the school relied on the Sinhalese government for funding, it had nothing. No desks, no chalk, no books. The sixty-eight children, all wearing perfectly pressed white uniforms, were clustered in the shadow of a tin over-hang, sitting on handkerchiefs that they had spread with great care. Only Vijay taught. There was one other teacher, but he hadn't shown up for ten weeks because the government had stopped paying him. Vijay had also not been paid, though he went home each night with both arms full of potatoes and beans and chickens, an occasional rupee, an occasional statue of a Hindu god.

98

We watched him teach. In this bleak, overcrowded setting with every imaginable obstacle to teaching, Vijay found a way to teach. He drew world maps in the dirt. He taught math by subtracting and adding students standing in front of the class. He acted the part of an elephant in a student drama of the *Ramayana*. Finally, using a goat's bladder stuffed with tea leaves as a soccer ball, he let students play soccer only after they correctly translated some English verbs.

My dad observed all of this very intently. "God bless that boy," he said, and said it in a way that indicated things inside of him were getting shook up. How minor must his own trials have now seemed when compared to the trials of these children, and to Vijay. "He's a magician, that's what he is. Out of nothing he creates so much. And look at those little girls over there, how much fun they're having and learning at the same time."

"He was trained by the Peace Corps," I said. "A lot of what he's doing is what I'm teaching my students up at Bandarawela. We improve their English, but mainly we teach them how to teach in primitive schools like this one. Vijay's a natural teacher, but without the ideas Peace Corps gave him, I think he'd be over-whelmed."

My dad nodded but had no reply. I tried to find in the slant of his head or the narrowing of his eyes some measure of validation for my work, but I found none. I told myself that it really didn't matter. And I repeated that it didn't matter, repeated it so often on our walk home up the mountain path—carrying Vijay's booty of mangoes and bread, passing the tea-pickers spitting betel juice into the tea fields—that I nearly came to believe my own lie.

On our last night at Vijay's house the three of us walked at dusk to the Hindu temple, the center of the tea estate community. Vijay knew everybody on the walk: the family of five riding on a bike, the old lady toting a small tree on her head, every tea-picker, every child. Out of respect for the white men they all stood to the side as we passed, looking down at the ground.

We smelled the temple long before we reached it. A thick cloud of incense had spread out from the gates and across the tea fields. When we arrived at the temple, the incense partly obscured our view of the statues on the roof, an astonishing array of colorful Hindu gods that were dancing or sitting or balancing on one foot. My dad marveled at them.

"Look at the monkey face," he said, "and the elephant. And that one with all those arms. Amazing, all this art in the middle of nowhere. Who paints these things, Vooji, and how often?"

Vijay answered these questions and more, patiently teaching my father about this new world of Hinduism. His curiosity surprised me. I had expected him to be repulsed by it all, to regard it as the kind of barbaric and pagan religion that Christianity ought to convert.

We placed our shoes outside the gate and entered the temple. The fifty or so Tamils didn't know where to look, either down at the ground as they had been taught, or up at this mesmerizing sight of two white men with blue eyes and hair on their arms. To them this must have been a miracle, two Americans come to worship in their temple here on their forgotten plantation. They crowded around us. One of the men handed my dad a coconut and, following his example, invited him to throw it against the lingam, a concrete phallic stump. My dad raised his eyebrows at the phallic business, but then wound up and hurled the coconut. It split open and its milk spattered on the stump, and the people rushed forward to touch it and taste it and spread it on the foreheads of their babies. I was waiting for my dad to make some derogatory swipe at all of this—"Bunch of apes, these people!"—but it never came. Instead he followed the lead of an old Hindu man and set a tray of bananas at the foot of Shiva.

The Hindu priest approached. He stood before my father in just a loincloth, his face and body streaked with ash. For a moment these two opposites stood eye to eye—a nearly naked holy man facing a white man in wool pants holding a Gatorade bottle—and I wondered what sense either could possibly make of the other.

The priest bowed low to my father and chanted some prayers. When he arose, he laced around my dad's neck a garland of brilliant red flowers. He then pressed his thumb into a bowl of golden dust and, reciting a prayer, dabbed a spot of yellow saffron on the center of my dad's forehead.

Vijay said to my father, "The priest is telling you that you are a god in his temple, that the god inside of you has met the god inside of him."

My dad appeared moved by this. He pressed his hands together in front of the garland and, bowing to the priest, said, "Wanacome."

The priest didn't appear surprised, but the rest of the crowd froze. This one holy Tamil word, *wanacome*, this mere puff of air out of my dad's mouth, had now become as sacred as incense. It settled softly on the heads of these maligned people, settling over their black faces and splendid saris, over their hands callused from picking tea. For a moment their hard lives were full of majesty, full of peace. For a moment that contained eternity, the vast distance from black to white, from Hindu to Catholic, from tea-picker to judge, from Sri Lanka to America—all was ultimately no further than the utterance of a word.

Later that night my father and I went to sleep in our twin beds. Though he had washed his face with water from the drum, my dad went to bed with the saffron dot still centering his forehead. The garland of red flowers leaned against his Gatorade bottle. I stared at those flowers for a long time, remembering the stories my father had told me on the long walk home from the temple: about selling apples during the Depression; about his own father, a detective, hunting down Al Capone; about asking a naked, dripping-wet Babe Ruth for his autograph; about his coming home from school one day to find a "quarantined" sign on his house, and how his only brother, Jimmy, and a sister, Virginia, died that night from scarlet fever.

The next morning we left Vijay's home. In an act that was not silly, my dad opened the left outhouse door and put his garland of flowers around the goat's neck. He said good-bye to the chickens and the cow, flicked the flies off the plastic fish just for fun, and pulled a strand of cane from the notorious chair and put it in his mouth, Huck Finn–style.

Outside, Vijay's sisters lined up on their knees. My father stood before each one, firmly touching each head with all his fingers. He accepted a packet of *wadee*s from Vijay's mother and an embrace from Vijay before starting to leave.

*Sir.*

We turned around. There, standing in the doorway with her hands pressed together, was the grandmother. She raised her eyes from the ground and said through Vijay's translation, "Sir, you have honored my family by coming here. You are old, and I know it is not easy for the old to learn the new. You are a good and holy man. May Krishna bless your many lives."

My dad approached her. The wind uplifted some strands of gray hair not covered by his Indians cap; it uplifted some strands of her gray hair not bound in a bun. These were the elders, standing in their own sacred circle. He bowed to her with his palms together, saying in a very familiar way, "Wanacome." She shook his hands and then hugged him, crying, her head somewhere at the level of his navel. And then, in a gesture of either comedy or sanctity, my dad placed his Indians cap on her head. Vijay and I laughed, but from her reaction you'd think she had just been crowned with a tiara of diamonds.

As we walked away she waved the cap up high, an old exuberant Tamil woman with rings in her nose, standing on the tips of her toes, waving an American baseball cap higher and higher until we turned a bend and were out of her sight forever.

We walked through the lemon grass, now a foot taller since we had first seen it a week earlier. Because of the high grass we missed the Tamil line house until, from above our heads, a boy shouted down to us.

"Wanacome!" We arched our necks and saw him waving from a tree branch. "Wanacome, wanacome!"

It was the boy who had run out with a mango for us. His father yelled to him from inside the house, probably ordering him to be quiet and to get down from that tree. But when my dad shouted "wanacome" back up to the boy, his father, carrying a baby on one shoulder and another child on a hip, stepped out of the house in wonder.

My dad waved to him, too, and shouted, "Wanacome."

More of the family emerged, and still more. They looked to the Tamil father to see what to do, and when he called out, "Wanacome," they did too. The boy above us kept repeating it and then threw an avocado down to me. An old lady in the doorway said, "Wanacome," then hid her toothless smile behind her apron. And off on her own in the shade of a tree, still rocking as she had a week earlier, the deformed girl lifted her twisted hand and gurgled her own form of "wanacome."

By this time a crowd had gathered in front of the house and throughout the tea fields. They stared at my father in awe, as if seeing a rare and fleeting marvel, like the passing of a blimp. My dad sang "wanacome" to them all and waved in every direction. This small action would now be the stuff of legend in this community of the oppressed. "Wanacome!" he repeated, twirling around. "Wanacome, everybody! Wanacome!"

And for each of his *wanacome*s came the echo of fifty others, encircling us, so that here on this hillside of tea at eye level with the clouds, I felt perched on the branch of a holy tree, surrounded by the song of a thousand swallows.

7

We should have left right then. I should have stolen enough money
from my father's thick wallet to hire a helicopter, airlifting him from
that hillside of tea back to his own Cleveland condominium. He'd
be back in his climate-controlled, noise-controlled, pest-controlled
bedroom, marveling at the dream he had just had: of a saffron dot,
of a wrinkled black woman waving his Indians cap, of a chorus of
*wanacome* fluttering around him like butterflies.

But instead we pressed on. Our bus to Kandy sputtered up the hill
towards us, leaning heavily, passing the taxi driver still asleep in his
cab. As usual the bus was packed both inside and out, the overflow of
people hugging the roof and clinging to the steps and the windows.
It was cruel of me to force my dad back in there. After all the demons
he had just faced—the flies, the cane chair, the goat in the outhouse,
the defiled left hand—he deserved to swing in a hammock between
two tall oaks, Betty Grable feeding him grapes one by one.

The bus stopped in front of us. In two years I had never seen
such a crush of humanity on a bus, and I knew this time that there
was absolutely no room anywhere for us. My father and I stepped
away from the bus, resigned that we'd have to figure something
else out. But then, miraculously, an aisle opened up for us from
the pavement all the way inside, leading us to a vacant bench near

the driver. There, an old man with betel-red gums was dusting off the bench for us with the hem of his sarong. I looked around. The old man and all the others on the bus were Tamils, and then it all made sense: This seat was a gift. I'm certain that every person on the bus knew that we had visited their school and temple, had slept in Vijay's bedroom, had chanted "wanacome" to the lowliest Tamils in the line house. And when the old man pounded the bench with his fist to show its sturdiness, I knew that the Cane Chair Plunge was common knowledge, too.

Outside our window we saw waterfalls and jungles, steep mountain canyons, monkeys, parrots, temples. The rays of the sun filtered through the thick monsoon clouds like the fingers of God, and when my father sighed "Ahhh" at the majesty of it all, so too did the old Tamil man, though he was not looking out the window. His eyes, like the hundred others on the bus, were locked onto my father and me, mesmerized by us celebrities who *wanted* to ride on their ragged bus rather than in a rented car. All of their faces looked old to me, even those of the young, but their eyes and smiles were childlike and radiant.

Out from the crowd stepped a little Tamil boy. Without any shyness he walked up to my father just to touch, and then to stroke, the gray hair on his forearms. My dad smiled at the touch. After a short while he began an old game with the boy that he had played often with me. He tightened his hand into a fist and shot out a random finger for the boy to grab. Immediately the boy knew the object of the game, and as he lunged and missed the finger over and over, the bus sang with laughter. Eventually the boy caught the finger, or my dad let him catch it, and when he did, everyone cheered. For the next half-hour the boy never let go of that finger.

"These finger games," my dad said to me, "sure work up a man's hunger." He pointed to the paper sack of *wadees* from Vijay's mother, a sack nearly transparent from the oil. "Maybe it's about time I tried one of those grease biscuits."

I handed him one. At first he ate it like a squirrel, holding the little *wadee* at the tips of his finger, nibbling nervously at the edges. Then, after studying the taste, he popped the whole thing into his mouth and said while chewing, "Not a bad little treat. Little crunchy but not bad at all."

By this time the little boy had had enough of just holding my dad's finger. He plunged it into his mouth, slobbering all over it.

"Tasty as a wadee, isn't it?" my father said to him.

But the boy disregarded him and just kept on sucking, and for the rest of the trip my dad let him do it. The sight brought a memory to me I had long forgotten: of me as a five-year-old playing with the green marble on the zipper of my father's ragged winter coat. We were searching for a Christmas tree, but all I cared about was that mesmerizing green marble. In the freezing cold I zipped it up and down, up and down, and annoying as it must have been, my father held me tight to his chest and let me do it.

In Kandy we unloaded ourselves like clowns in a magic act, body after body after improbable body from a bus built to carry one-fourth of us. Nearby a hundred Tamils bowed to us, saying "Wanacome," while off to the side the little Tamil boy stood in tears, his arms wrapped tightly around his own father's leg.

My dad and I turned to face the chaos of an overpopulated city. I scanned the crowd for Cindy but saw only tour guides and beggars ready to pounce on our white skin. Once our feet were on the ground they stampeded toward us.

"Taxi, sir! Taxi cheap to temple!"

"Sir wants hotel? So cheap, my friend, come come come with—"

"Tours for the sir?"

"I hungry, sirs. No eat, never eat. Ten children, betty betty hungry, no eat. Sir, one rupee, sir . . ."

They were upon us. My dad said "wanacome" to many of them

until I told him that this Tamil word no longer had any meaning in this Sinhalese, Buddhist world. But I don't think he was listening. I think he was longing for the lemon grass and the tea fields and the solitude up at Vijay's, all now replaced by the clamor of horns and voices, the soldiers with menacing looks, the diesel exhaust and Fanta bottles, the piles of garbage everywhere that cats and crows and cows rooted through.

At the center of this disorder rose Sri Lanka's holiest shrine, the sprawling Temple of the Tooth, which attracts Buddhist pilgrims and tourists from around the world. The simplicity and austerity associated with Buddhism are nowhere in sight at this temple. All is gold. Beneath a gold roof behind gold doors within a gold vault rests Buddha's left bicuspid, brought to Sri Lanka from India in the fourth century concealed in a princess's hair. Where there is religion there often is war, and plenty of wars were fought and many empires made over that tooth. Today, the tooth remains within the innermost of seven bell-shaped reliquaries, all of pure gold and ornamented with precious gems. For two weeks in August a replica of the reliquary is paraded around the streets of Kandy in Sri Lanka's most spectacular festival, the Perahera, a chaotic night-parade of fire-eaters and dancers and a hundred elephants lit like Christmas trees.

"Sir, to temple I take."

"You ride my elephant, sir. Betty betty cheap, my friend."

"Gold teeth for sale, betty cheap."

"One rupee, sir. I no eat for one week, sir. I hungry, sir."

This entire scene stopped annoying me the moment I saw Cindy. She ran to meet us, dodging cows and beggars and a swarm of people until she stood face to face with my father and me. I didn't sweep her up in my arms or kiss or hug her. The best we could do in Sri Lanka, a land that discourages displays of affection on the street, was to link our pinky fingers. We did, and they stayed linked while my dad filled her in on our week with Vijay. She kept interrupting him for more details, like how the goat came to be named "Malone" and what Vijay was going to do with Ranji. Eventually, I suggested that we move away from this bus depot and visit the Temple of the Tooth.

"Not yet," Cindy said. "I've lined up Jewel with her gem dealer. Let's go take care of that sapphire business so I won't have to see her face again for a very long time. Are you up for it, John?"

He would never be up for it, but he knew he had to satisfy my mom's demand to buy her a blue sapphire. "Bring me a rock, John," she told him. "One that will knock out Peggy Malone's eyes. Make it a sapphire. And make it big."

Such a mission terrified him. To make this type of large purchase in a culture without fixed prices aroused in him the fear of being made a fool. Some greasy shyster might sell him a worthless bauble of glass and then later, with his drunken buddies, howl over the gullible old American in wool pants. To my dad the entire world was mined with such dangers: America had its Nebraska Coke machines, Sri Lanka had its corrupt gem dealers.

"Lil," he had told my mom before leaving, "can't I get you one of these sapphire things here? Cleveland's got all kinds of gem stores. Reliable ones. Fair ones. I have friends who—"

"Get it there, John. And get it big. I don't want Peggy looking down at my finger and seeing just a pimple."

"But Lil—"

"Just get it, John."

So we set out to complete this dirty work. We checked into a hotel and waited on the balcony for Jewel and her gem entourage. At the knock on the door my dad tensed up, twirling the loose band of his wristwatch around and around. Cindy rose to let them in.

Jewel's booming voice preceded her entrance onto the balcony. "What a day, what a day, oh lordy lordy, little Cindy, what a day. First, I git myself on the bus, see, and then . . . Oh, why hey there, Judge! My oh my I'll have to git myself up to Ohio if they grows 'em all as perty as you." She shook my dad's limp hand in hers, solid and tight, and continued. "So, there I am on the bus, see, puts my sack of coconuts in the overhead, and after a couple of minutes ridin' in one a them deathtraps they dare call a 'bus,' here they come tumbling: boing, boing, boing! All three of my coconuts, they falls kerplunk square on my noggin. Then I gits off the bus woozy as a drunk and whadya know, I steps square in a load of cow shit. How's that for a good mornin'?"

My dad stared at Jewel and twirled his watch.

Behind her stood the gem dealers, Ranjith and his wife, Manjula, both dressed in Western clothes. Ranjith carried a shaving kit beneath his arm, its leather flaked and peeling, from which he pulled out handfuls of white paper squares folded like drug packets. His watch, I noticed, was running three hours slow.

"The balcony is a lovely place to view my treasures," Ranjith smiled. "The sunlight, you understand, must . . . *dazzle* and irradiate these blessings of the earth."

"Bring 'em on out, Ronny," Jewel said, holding a cigarette between two crooked and yellowed fingers. "Bring 'em out and do your soft shoe, fella'. Just don't blind these kind folks with all that dazzle now, ya hear. Maybe we oughta sell 'em sunglasses first, eh Ronny?"

Ranjith's head shot back with a roaring laugh. "Oh, Miss Jewel, Miss Jewel. How . . . *delightful!*"

She turned to Manjula. "Honey, whadya say you run along and get ol' Jewel a beer. Beer never hurt nobody, specially on the equator." She fanned her face with her hand, wafting her cigarette smoke over to my face. "Goddamn, it's hot! Time to hit up ol' J. C. Penney for some air conditioners."

My dad, gnawing on his lower lip, crossed and then recrossed his legs.

"And Manjula," Ranjith added, "bring up whatever my good American friends here would like. Beer? Scotch? You name the—ha-ha!—the poison."

Jewel laughed mightily, her bullhorn cackle pushing at my head like a truck's heavy horn. "Hey-hey-hey, now that's the spirit, Ronny. In fact, Manny, bring me up a couple while you're at it. Save you a trip later."

My dad took a long sip from Big Green and checked the time. He wiped his forehead with his handkerchief and checked the time again.

Cindy pulled up her chair. "Jewel, let's not stretch this out," she said firmly. Her harsh tone reassured me that Cindy would be doing our dirty work for us. She could intimidate. She brought down the price of everything—bananas, candles, taxi fares—and I was confident she would do the same with sapphires. "Show us your best sapphire at a fair price and let's be done with it."

Jewel exhaled her smoke high into the air. "You got an appointment or somethin', Missy?"

"I just don't see the point of dragging this whole circus out."

"Seems to me you ain't the one with the purse strings, young lady. That good-lookin' judge is doing the buying, so hows about you give ol' Manny a hand with them beers? Make yourself useful, Missy, and run along. Go ahead: run along."

Cindy turned to Ranjith. "Let's see the goods."

After a little confusion he opened up his white packets, each containing about ten gems, and before we could stop him he had opened up twenty more. My antennae rose. Hadn't I seen this selling technique before, this burst of work that obligated the buyer to purchase something? I remembered the Moroccan bazaar I had entered as a college student. A slick merchant with a pinky ring and oily hair lured me into his shop to buy a Persian rug, perhaps the most superfluous item on the planet for a young student living on cheese. Within seconds rugs unfurled from high stacks, one after another. "Ahh, my friend, just look, just look. No charge to look." More and more rugs, and as I sipped mint tea cross-legged, and as a brown siren fanned me with a palm, I came to appreciate the color and the craft of these rugs, now piled higher than my eyes.

Yes, I agreed, this *was* an investment, and this *was* the start of an heirloom for my children's grandchildren, and this *was* a steal of a price. Why yes, I'd love more tea and yes, if you don't mind, could you fan this side of me? One hundred dollars—that's *all!*—and the other hundred when the rug arrives in Ohio. Where do I sign?

The rug never came, of course, which over time became my own private Nebraska Coke machine.

Jewel sipped her beer. "Hey, Ronny, this here's a judge, so hows about we forget the iddy-biddy pebble shit and get to the big casabas. His old lady wants to show off the rock in Palm Beach, ain't that the truth, your Honor?"

"Big casabas?"

"That's right, Judgey. The big guns. Let's start 'em up at five grand."

"Five—!"

"No sense fiddlin' with pebbles."

"Pebbles might work."

"You bring home a pebble, Judge, and your little white ass is grass. Take it from a lady."

My dad said nothing more, slouching lower in his chair, twirling his watch as if unscrewing his wrist. I'm sure that he imagined going to a Cleveland jeweler with his blue pebble to assess its value. The jeweler would lower his eyepiece and say gravely, "What you have here, sir, is a ten-cent piece of blue glass. And you paid . . . what did you say, *five thousand dollars!* Really, in all of my years in the gem business—and I don't mean any disrespect here, sir—this is by far the stupidest thing I've ever heard anyone do. You'd expect a mistake like this from a child, or a beagle. But never, no, never a judge."

My dad was running out of chair to slouch down into.

"Hey, Jewel!" It was Cindy, her eyes narrowed and raging. "Knock it off, all of it! We asked you to come here with a guy we could trust and all I've seen so far is a bunch of crooks running up a bar bill on John's tab."

"Oh, Cindy dear, I never in all my glorious life—"

"Our ceiling is three hundred dollars. We want the best sapphire you've got or else we'll—"

"Honey, there ain't no sense being tight as a frog's ass at a time like this."

"Knock it off, Jewel! Let's cut to the chase or we'll call up one of the thousand guys out there selling sapphires."

Ranjith looked at Jewel, shrugged, and unfolded another handful of packets. "I understand your fears, my American friends," he said, "but Ranjith and deception are no bedfellows. Understand that. Here are sapphires, all for three hundred dollars, that will fetch ten times that price in your great land of plenty. That is a proven fact. Here, here is one"—his tweezers pinched a sapphire—"that in my right mind I should sell for three, maybe five thousand dollars, but for you, my dear friends of my dear friend Miss Jewel E. Jewel, I will close my eyes and take a horrible loss at three hundred dollars. Just don't tell my competitors. They will make a laughing stock of me. They will call me"—he chuckled—"'Dumbo the Clown.'"

Jewel lowered her beer, licking off the white mustache of foam across her lip. "You're a prince, Ronny. With a capital 'P.' And that there sappeer is a doozy. Snatch this one up, Judgey, before Ronny comes to his senses."

Cindy held the stone by the tweezers up to the sun.

My dad leaned toward me. "Say, Jim," he whispered, "sounds like a terrific deal. Looks big and three hundred clams, that sounds sweet to me." His fingers moved toward the buttons guarding his money pouch.

I agreed, delighted that we Toner men had stood up to these crooks.

Ranjith started folding the packets and placing some in his shaving kit. "'Dumbo' will without doubt be my new name. Well, it is a small price to pay for friendship from sea to shining sea. Just tell your friends to come find Dumbo. Now, Manjula, there will be no 'Dumbo' from you."

"Oh, Miss Jewel," Manjula giggled, "shall we call him 'Dumbo' from now on?"

"He's a 'Dumbo' sure as shit. Hey, Judge, that'll be cash or traveler's checks? Dumbo here's partial to the greenbacks, if it ain't no matter to you."

"Oh, cash is—"

Cindy tossed the sapphire onto the table like a dead bug. "It has a crack," she announced. "Right through the middle."

The room fell silent. A monkey screeched from a nearby tree.

For a minute the tension in the air thickened, then Ranjith, then Manjula, then Jewel—they all began laughing. "That 'crack,' as you call it," Ranjith said, "is a rare imperfection found only in Ratnapura sapphires. That 'crack'"—more laughter; they were having the time of their lives—"has just tripled the value of your gem. My heartfelt congratulations, my dear friends."

"Tripled!" my dad beamed.

"Maybe more," Ranjith said.

Jewel raised her beer. "Judge, you just got yourself a happy wife and a happy banker. I'm so tickled I could up and do a jig."

"Dumbo, Dumbo, Dumbo," Manjula laughed. "Ranjith the Dumbo."

"Yes: I am guilty of being a Dumbo."

Cindy stood up. "But it ruins the stone. That 'valuable crack' ruins it completely. It's worthless."

Ranjith held the tweezers up high to the sun. "Not if you have the right light, madam. Look. Notice what we in the business call 'dazzle.' Notice the dazzling dazzle, but be careful. Maybe as Miss Jewel says, you need sunglasses." His chuckle was now slight and unnatural. "What I hold in my hand is a valuable stone, madam, and if you think I am deceiving you, I will find my temper grow apoplectic and then in good conscience I will pack up my treasures and—"

My dad nudged me. "Tell her to back off a bit," he insisted under his breath.

"I can't."

"You can't? What do you mean you can't?"

"I just can't. She'll get . . . I don't know, angry at me."

"Oh, for God's sake!"

Jewel stood. "Anyone for a beer?"

"Take a seat, Jewel," Cindy ordered. "I don't suppose it's news to you that your friend is trying to cheat us."

Jewel, gasping, pointed a yellow finger at Cindy's eyes. "You are one foolish young lady, Missy. And I suggest you address your elders with a bit more respect. In Arkansas we have a name for your kind but since I'm a lady I won't pollute my mouth by utterin' it."

"Take a hike, Jewel."

Ranjith raised his hand. "With all due respect to you, Miss Cindy, this is my business and Miss Jewel is my dazzling friend. For thirty years I have sold thousands of gems, and so I know that this . . . this *crack*, adds what we gem scientists call 'luster.'"

"You heard the man, Missy," Jewel said. "The rock's full of lusser. Manny, be a dear and call up room service for a round."

My dad whispered to Cindy, "Maybe we ought to rethink this. After all, three hundred dollars is a—"

"It's a scam, John. Believe me, it's practically worthless."

Ranjith moved his chair nearer to my father. "My friend, she is a lovely daughter but this is my business. Last offer: two hundred and fifty dollars, and that is only because you are my friend."

Cindy began folding his last packets for him. "I've had enough of that 'friend' crap, Ranjith. It's time to hit the road."

"Last offer: two hundred dollars. To go lower would be a crime."

"You're a shyster."

"One hundred and fifty dollars. Period."

"Here's twenty—John, peel him off a twenty—and that's as a favor."

"Ohhhh no no no, my friend, I cannot—"

"You can and you will and for the last time I'm not your friend. Take the twenty and give me the cracked junk sapphire or I'll show you the door *now!*"

A mustache of sweat formed above his lip. Manjula uncrossed her legs then crossed them again while Jewel hummed into her beer. The monkey's screech pierced the room like an arrow.

Ranjith nodded. "Yes, with sadness I accept. But only if you'd be interested in buying a few of these moonstone earrings, a delicate little jewel that—"

"Give it up, Ranjith. One stone, one twenty."

He wiped away the sweat mustache with the back of his hand, passed over the packet, and then zipped shut his shaving kit.

"And Jewel," Cindy said, "before you run along with your friends, those beers'll cost you two hundred rupees."

Jewel's face sagged. "Lord in glorious heaven I never—"

"And if you don't have it with you, which you probably don't, I'll get the Peace Corps office to take it out of your next paycheck."

"You," Jewel said, pointing her charred fingertip, "are nastier than a trapped hog. Lord in heaven I place my pity on your poor husband's head. Jim, take the advice of a Arkansas lady and run for the hills, far far away from this here polecat. Today, Missy, today you've embarrassed my friends and"—Cindy guided her by the elbow out the door and down the corridor—"and and and let me tell you it's a goddamn good thing my nails is bit to the nub or by sweet Jesus if my name ain't Jewel E. Jewel I'd go for your eyes, sure as shit!"

On the balcony, meanwhile, the two Toner lads leaned back in their chairs, hands behind their heads, proud that they had stood up to these crooks.

"That'll teach them to mess with Americans, eh Dad?"

"Ohio justice. That's what they got a dose of today, Jimmy. Ohio justice."

"We sure knocked 'em to their knees."

"Ohio justice'll do that, Jimmy. It takes no prisoners." He held his twenty-dollar sapphire up to the sun, turning it to find the crack. "I'll tell Lil it cost me a bundle and she won't know the difference. Just you watch. She'll stick it under Peggy Malone's nose first chance she gets." He tucked the gem into his waist pouch. For a long time he gazed out at the aralia trees and the golden reflection of the Temple of the Tooth on the lake in front of it. He leaned forward to watch the monkeys swinging like acrobats from banyan tree to banyan tree, and then he watched the elephants loping along the road. "It just feels a little bit funny," he said after a while. "Your mother won't know but I'll know and well, it feels a little bit funny. I keep thinking about that old lady up at Vijay's, his grandmother, and how happy she was when I gave her a cheap little baseball cap. Remember her face, Jimmy? Remember that smile? I bet she wouldn't trade that beat-up old hat of mine for a sack full of sapphires."

The next day we passed Kandy Lake on our walk to the Temple of the Tooth. Cindy, her eyes alert to the details of nature that I always missed, pointed out to us the snakes among the reeds, the pelicans, the turtles, the turquoise kingfishers on the branches overhanging the water. My dad said that the brilliant colors of those birds reminded him of Popsicles.

In the trees above us a few crows cawed. I told my dad that at dusk the trees were so packed with crows and bats that pedestrians used umbrellas to protect themselves from the droppings.

"I doubt there's *that* many," he said.

We saw a few monkeys making their circus leaps from tree to

tree, saw another snake, saw two Buddhist monks get into a black Mercedes. An elephant chained at the ankles approached us carrying a tree trunk in its snout, its long penis dangling so openly that none of us knew quite what to say.

As we approached the temple the beggars began to thicken, for this was prime real estate full of sympathetic people. On the outer edge they weren't so bad, poor and tattered but all limbs intact. But the cases worsened near the temple gates. With a mix of horror and fascination my dad stared at the girl with a partial face, at the blind woman without a nose, at the man with tiny flippers for limbs. We passed a boy with elephantiasis, his legs grotesquely swollen and lifeless. My dad tried to avert his eyes from those legs but couldn't, so mesmerized was he by the agony and decay of a live human body. A dog moved away from a pile of rubbish to sniff the swollen leg, and the boy hadn't the will to shoo it away.

My dad unzipped his waist pouch. "Give him whatever is a lot here, Jimmy." He handed me a wad of money, causing many other beggars to incline toward me. "And where are the doctors here? Why isn't that boy in a hospital?"

"Some people just see it as their fate," Cindy said. "They believe they lived rotten lives in the past and are paying for it now."

"That's a load of rubbish, if you ask me. You tell me about all the gold on that roof and all the gold around a little tooth and here, by God, these people are *suffering*."

"Well, Dad, you know the Catholic Church is no different. How many billions of dollars in gold do you suppose the Vatican has in . . ."

But he wasn't listening to me. He was staring at a man sitting on the ground with his back against the temple gates, his entire body so hunched that his long knotted beard touched the cement. The black stain on his thigh was not, as we first thought, a discoloration of the skin. It was flies, hundreds of them, rising in a black, buzzing cloud as we passed. In the moment before they settled back down on the leg, we could see through the wide and bloody cavity right down to the man's thigh bone.

"I need to sit," my dad said, his hand covering his mouth. "I need to sit right now."

He did. And as other tourists approached, some recording all of these beggars on their video cameras, they paused at this improbable last sight: an ashen old white man holding a Totes umbrella and a Gatorade bottle. One German tourist filmed his wife dropping a ten-rupee note onto my dad's lap.

We took off our shoes at the temple gates, paying someone five rupees to keep an eye on them. I had never seen a shoe guardian at any other Sri Lankan temple, nor had I ever seen someone offer to help white barefoot tourists across the sharp stones to the temple entrance—for ten rupees. A Buddhist monk sold tickets for fifty rupees to ride an "authentic Perahera elephant." To have your picture taken next to the elephant cost twenty rupees. To pet the elephant cost five rupees. These and other options were spelled out on a sign written in five languages. On the bottom it read, "Blessings by monk free. We like donations."

I hated having my father see Buddhism in this way, though he may have been too concerned with the pebbles digging into the soles of his feet to notice. His were not Sri Lankan feet, leathery and webbed and elastic, but tender suburban feet accustomed to the thick protection of wing tips. My dad leaned heavily on my arm, wincing. A couple of soldiers, seeing my dad wobble and grimace, grinned and aimed their guns at his feet as if pretending to shoot him into a dance.

Inside the temple the cool marble floor comforted my dad's feet. The coolness surprised him.

"Are there frozen pipes beneath here?" he asked. "You know, pipes like they have running under skating rinks."

I asked if he was joking.

"About what?" he asked.

"About those frozen pipes, here, in the middle of the jungle."

"What pipes?"

"The ones you just talked about, the frozen ones."

His attention turned to the soft murmur of a hundred meditators, leaving me with the clear sense that senility was not too far down the road for my father. The meditators sat cross-legged in front of a colossal Buddha reclining along the length of the temple, his robe bright orange, his eyelids half-closed. I handed my dad a flower to place with all the others stacked in front of the statue. He raised the flower to his nose.

"Oh, no," I said, grabbing his arm. "Don't sniff."

"Don't sniff what?"

"The flower."

"I'm not blowing my nose on it."

"But just to smell it is to defile it. It's their custom, that's all. It would be like offering that disgusting snot rag of yours to Buddha."

"My handkerchief?"

I told him that "handkerchief" was too elegant a word to describe the crinkly thing that always fell out of his back pocket. Whenever he asked me as a child to go get it out of the car, I'd pinch it by a thread on the edge, holding it at arm's length as if it were a dead rat.

"It just seems a bit extreme to me, that's all," he said. "We have noses to smell and flowers smell good."

"Dad, you'd be bugged, too, if a Sri Lankan broke one of your Catholic customs. Imagine if one of them took a communion host and rolled it down the aisle like a Necco wafer."

"A what?"

A Necco wafer was a round candy the size of a quarter that we pretended was a communion host when we were kids. I told my father that I used to play the priest, solemnly placing Neccoes on all my friends' tongues. "Then, Dad, we'd have the Necco fall out of our mouths and onto the ground and then we'd all pretend to be struck by lightning. George, Joe, Cogs, me—we'd all plop on the ground, fried."

This blasphemy beneath his own roof was more than my dad needed to know. I was relieved when out of nowhere a family of Sri Lankans invited us to their house for lunch. Cindy translated the offer to my dad.

"Well, isn't that something," he said, smiling. "Just like that, a bunch of strangers asking us into their home. Amazing! Tell them in America we don't go in for that kind of thing. Over there you invite a stranger inside and next thing you know, you got a slit throat. Tell them that."

Cindy did not tell them that. Instead, she tried to thank them for the lunch offer, but the sound of a deep, protracted gong in the center of the temple had turned their attention. It was time, they told us, for the event that everyone had come here for: the opening of the inner sanctum that held the Buddha's tooth. The family bowed and trotted away, their bare feet slapping on the marble.

The entire temple stirred. Hundreds of worshipers, many of whom had traveled days in packed buses for this moment, crushed against the railing that guarded the sanctum. At this thrilling and sacred moment my father pulled me aside.

"My tootsies," he said, "are getting a wee bit chilled."

"Your what?"

"My toesies. This marble, it's numbing my toes. Only frozen pipes could make a floor so cold."

We pressed against the back of the crowd, our heads at least a foot above everybody else's. A pudgy Buddhist monk appeared in front. He prayed to the golden door leading to the sanctum before turning to pray to the crowd, and then, seeing us, clapped his hands above his head and waved us forward. A thousand black Sri Lankan heads swiveled to see us. The monk clapped again, and as if on cue the crowd parted to allow us to pass to the front. My dad smiled at this special treatment, but I knew better. I knew that at the end of this "special treatment" would be a fat monk holding out his fat hand for some cash.

"Oh Lord in heaven," my dad said, walking up the aisle, "wait'll I tell Lil about this. And Malone! Malone would kill to be here."

The monk held his arms out wide like a peep-show huckster, a fancy and accurate watch glittering at the edge of his robe. "My friends, my friends," he said to us in English. "Step right up here, my special friends, and as gift from my humble country come in where only special guests can come. You German?"

"American," my dad said. "Good old U. S. of A. Cleveland, to be exact. That's near Chicago, on the North Coast, or at least that's—"

"American!" exclaimed the monk. "Then you must know my very good friend Robert Davis in California."

"Davis . . . Davis . . . Davis. . . ," my dad said. I couldn't believe that he was actually running through the directory in his brain for a Robert Davis. "No, but there is an Ozzie Davis out there. Married to Harriet."

"Perhaps you know him by 'Bob.' 'Bob Davis.' He is a very handsome man."

"Well, there is an Al Davis out there. Runs a football team. Are you sure it's not Ozzie? He's a handsome fellow, too, but come to think of it I'm pretty sure he's dead."

The monk sighed as if touched by Ozzie's death. His grief ended when another monk escorted two German couples, both with camcorders, into our group. Our monk asked one of the Germans about a Hans in Frankfurt.

This went on for some time. Eventually the monk opened the massive gold door and led us into the red-carpeted inner sanctum. The crowd of Sri Lankans surged forward, restrained by the barricade and by a line of soldiers. The two German men pivoted like gunslingers onto their knees and, adjusting eye to eyepiece, filmed the onrushing Sri Lankans as if sighting panthers in the wild.

The two-ton door shut behind us with the thud of a bank vault. One of the Germans behind a camcorder waved the monk closer toward the bed of red velvet on which rested the gold chest containing Buddha's tooth. The monk smiled, his round cheeks reflecting the overhead lights. "Please," he said to the camera, "let me stand over here. I believe my right side is my better side."

Cindy pinched my dad's arm. "Let's get out of here."

"Oh, not yet," my dad said. "Imagine! To be this close to where no one ever gets and boy! I could kick myself for not getting one of those movie things before I left. I should listen to Malone, that's for sure."

"Dad, you can't be serious," I said. "It's a show, it's a scam. Just remember that garland of flowers from the Hindu priest. And the saffron dot on your forehead."

He didn't reply. Meanwhile, all around us were more pictures, more poses, more bouncy and frivolous banter. "Ohhhhh, yes," the monk said, "I *love* Bavarian sausage. And *sauerkraut!* Oh, it is my dream to some day go to your Oktoberfest."

I closed my eyes.

And I prayed: "Dear God, look down on us with all your Old Testament wrath. Look down on us seven hefty Aryans inside this sanctum which a thousand worthy Sri Lankans beyond that door could never enter. Look down on us and on this paunchy monk living the luxurious life courtesy of our cash. Look on us, on all of us, gaping at a hunk of gold that could contain Buddha's toenail or petrified shit as easily as his tooth. Take all of this scene, God, and in all of your power start spinning this room like the Rotor at Cedar Point. Spin it so fast that it sucks us to the walls—faster, faster—and the floor drops beneath us so that we cling to the walls—faster! faster still!—and the saffron robe of the monk flies in a gust above his head to show his soft thighs and belly and balls all jiggling from decades of idleness. Let chunks of Bavarian sausage come vomiting out of every German's mouth. O God, let us spin ever faster, lifting this chamber off from the cold marble floor with freezing pipes rupturing, lifting over the heads of the worshiping Sri Lankans who are at first terrified then astonished then amused at us. Give each of them a camcorder, God, and a waist pouch bursting with rupees. And a leather reclining chair for every bus passenger. Amen."

When I opened my eyes nothing had changed. A German man was filming his wife shaking a fistful of deutsche marks into the monk's hand. Outside the thick golden door I could hear the low hum of the thousand Sri Lankans murmuring their prayers. And inside I could hear something else.

"Get me out of here, Jimmy," my father said.

The monk overheard this. He stepped away from the babbling Germans and, in a gesture that surprised me, bowed low to my father. Upon rising, the monk smiled as if proud of some achievement, as if this is what he'd wanted all along: not a fistful of money, but a roomful of Westerners ready to scream. Suddenly it all made perfect sense to me. Perhaps the monk was no shyster after all, but a teacher, and this entire scene in the temple—the wave into the inner sanctum, the English, the watches, the poses, the unholy banter—was an elaborate morality play he'd designed to test our souls. The man was a genius. All he needed to seduce us inside and to keep us inside was to dangle our strongest temptation in front of our eyes: that of being the Chosen Ones. He had made us feel complicit in our own corruption. And now, standing aside to let us feel either repulsed or pleased, he left it up to us to decide what to do next. That was the test.

"Please, Jimmy," my dad repeated, his eyes blazing, "get me out of here *now*."

8

We left Kandy as quickly as possible. The bus to our friends'
house was crowded and rickety—what else is new—and in order
to breathe we all had to suck upwards like a pondful of carp. But
this time the bus experience felt different, and by the expression on
my dad's face I knew it was different for him, too. After the cracked
sapphire, after the prestige of white skin, after the camcorders and
the watches and the gold heaped on gold—after all that, it was a
relief to return to the rattle and the sway of the bus. There is no
deception, and there is no privilege, on a Sri Lankan bus. Here my
father shared the same burdens as everyone else, and in the process
discovered this truth: There is more reason to fear the roominess
of an inner sanctum than the crush on a bus of a hundred dark
bodies. In the same way, there is more reason to fear *Wheel of Fortune*
and Peggy Malone's sapphire than a *wadee*, than a saffron dot, than
a Tamil child's spit on a finger.

It began to rain once we got off the bus. At first it fell lightly like
a mist, so all the colors that we saw—the green of the banana trees,
the yellow of the rice shafts, the white of the Buddhist temple—
were lightened toward gray. We turned our faces up to the thick
monsoon clouds. My father opened his mouth wide, drinking rain.

And then the clouds burst. For a while my dad kept his face up-turned, drinking and laughing, while Cindy and I stepped off the path in search of a banana tree for shelter. But when the raindrops began to drive into my dad's cheeks like pellets, he pulled out his Totes umbrella and struggled to open it. Cindy and I snapped off broad banana leaves to cover our heads, and when I saw my dad's white umbrella open and then invert from the strong winds, I snapped off a leaf for him, too.

We ran. The three of us sidestepped the puddles, our leaves held at an angle against the driving rain.

"It works!" my dad shouted. "This leaf thing, it really works!"

From somewhere ahead of us in the rain we heard two little girls. "Uncle Jim!" they screamed. "Auntie Cindy! Sudu Tatta!" And then we saw them, ten-year-old Lakshmi and seven-year-old Rufi, the daughters of our best Sri Lankan friends, Yaseratne and his wife, Sarala. The girls were running to meet us, stopping to jump into every puddle with both feet. Lakshmi skipped and Rufi did a handstand and each tried to steal the banana leaf of the other. They sprinted the last few yards toward us and jumped into the arms of Cindy and me, squeezing us tight and saying in Sinhala, *I love you, Uncle Jim. I love you, Auntie Cindy.* While Lakshmi would not let go of Cindy, Rufi jumped down from me and opened her arms upward toward "Sudu Tatta," her white father. *I love you, Sudu Tatta,* she said, and my dad let fall his banana leaf and hoisted her thin body onto his shoulders.

"Up up you go," he said. "Up on the big white horse."

Unable to hold her for long, he lowered Rufi to the ground and held both her and Lakshmi's hands. Together through the driving rain they ran, their tiny hands held firmly within his, running and playing with the water of the air, running as if running toward the waves of the sea.

Yaseratne and Sarala met us at their door with towels, apolo-gizing in Sinhala for the rain. Before they were even introduced Yaseratne was drying my father's hair and offering him one of his own dry shirts. He was a kind man. Among his kindnesses to me was the time I lay in agony with dengue fever, an illness aptly called "the bonecrusher disease." For three days he spoon-fed me and cooled my forehead with damp cloths, and when I realized he had been holding my hand for a long time, I broke down crying—crying just from the kindness of it all.

With everybody dry, it was time for the formal welcome. The family lined up in front of my father and, pressing their hands together, bowed low and said together, "Ayubowan."

A few weeks earlier at the airport my father had left my own *ayubowan* hanging limply in the air. But now that he knew the power of a single word, *wanacome*, he was eager to learn this Buddhist greeting for "the god in me greets the god in you."

It wasn't easy. Like Jewel E. Jewel, and maybe like all old people, my dad needed mental pictures to remember a word. The only way Jewel could remember the Sinhalese word for Thursday, *Brahaspatinda*, was for her to picture a "bra on a horsie named Patinda." In the same way, my dad could only remember *ayubowan* by picturing an eyeball with a bow-tie holding a wand. He drew this image on a scrap of paper while Yaseratne's family waited. He studied the paper, put it behind his back, studied it again, and then said, "Eyeballwand."

Eventually he got it, and when he did he wouldn't stop saying it. He *ayubowan*ed the family again and again, *ayubowan*ed the cat and the clouds, and *ayubowan*ed their mangy dog, Arrow, that ran to greet us. But suddenly at the sight of Arrow, Cindy hid behind me and then ran indoors. The family didn't understand, for Arrow was harmless and knew us well. I explained that recently a rabid dog at a temple had bitten deep into Cindy's arm and leg, and now she was afraid of dogs. Sarala covered her mouth at this news and ran inside with the girls to find Cindy.

*Where did she get the medicine?* Yaseratne asked me. *Sri Lanka has no rabies medicine, we have no penicillin. None for many months now.*

I knew what he was talking about, and I knew the embarrassing place this conversation was about to go. The civil war had kept all ships offshore, even medical supply ships, so Sri Lankans were dying of treatable diseases like rabies and malaria. But not us Americans. That Peace Corps line about being "one with the people" only works until you get dog spit in your veins. In an instant after getting bit, Cindy and I became the American elite. We hired a cab at New York prices to drive us at midnight through a curfew, driving past columns of flaming tires and past soldiers insisting on seeing Cindy's thigh wounds. Eventually we reached the only place in Sri Lanka with rabies vaccine, the American Embassy in Colombo. The Marines nodded to us at the gate, and then door after door opened for us, the privileged white Americans. Inside the infirmary Cindy got her golden medicine, as I would get mine in a few months for malaria. With the gold in our veins we returned through all those doors and waved to the Marines before returning to our village, smiling and healthy. In place of that illness, though, was the more malignant one of hypocrisy, which we tried our best to ignore.

The hypocrisy didn't escape Yaseratne. He nodded politely during the story but gradually his eyes left mine to stare far out across the valley. The rain had stopped and patches of fog were hanging low to the ground. Yaseratne pulled a nugget of betel out of his pocket and began chewing. At the words "American Embassy" he turned to the side and spat red juice. When I finished, his only remark was to ask my father if he wanted to try a chew. To my surprise he accepted.

"Did this as a kid," my dad said, inserting the folded leaf under his lip. "Did it with tobacco. Kept my mouth wet playing baseball on the sandlots."

It didn't take long for him to spit it all out and run indoors calling for water. This left Yaseratne and me alone, the rabies story still hanging between us like bus exhaust. He pointed down to my leg.

*You might want to do something about that,* he said.

There on my ankle bloated with blood to the size of a thumb was the thing I most loathed in Sri Lanka: a leech.

*Yaseratne, rip it off! Rip it off!*

He seemed pleased by all of this, as if saying, "Hey, Bigshot, where's your embassy now?" He lit a match and leaned down, burning the leech off of my leg and then kicking it into the high grass. He put his arm around my shoulder.

*Come, Jim,* he said. *Let's go get some tea.*

Inside the kitchen my dad was asking Sarala all sorts of questions: How does she start her fire, grate her coconut, clean the rice? How does she iron clothes without electricity? Was her marriage arranged? What was that like for her at first?

*It was paradise,* Yaseratne interrupted. *She got the most beautiful man in the world. Isn't that right, Sarala?*

*Yes, until Arrow came along. Now, please,* she said, waving us outside, *all of you go and let me cook or we'll never eat tonight.*

Yaseratne stayed to help her while the rest of us—Cindy and I in sarongs, Lakshmi and Rufi in saris, my dad in wool pants—sat on the porch drinking our tea. The sun was setting and the air was wet, two conditions that brought the mosquitoes out in swarms. While my dad kept asking questions to the children, like if their feet got sore on the walk to school and if they played with Tamils, Cindy spread on his neck and back an Avon beauty product, Skin So Soft, which by chance repelled mosquitoes. It was standard Peace Corps issue. At any gathering of international volunteers, you could always locate the Peace Corps table simply by their Avon smell.

We were all enjoying our leisurely tea except for Rufi. She kept pulling on my dad's arm with all her might, begging him to come play red light, green light with her. Lakshmi, who liked sitting with the adults, told her sister to relax and sit but the tugging went on. My dad finally jumped up.

"Let's play," he said. "I'll be 'it' first."

The five of us walked to a clearing in the center of the yard. We watched the bats slashing across the sky and then listened to the Muslim call for prayer coming from loudspeakers across the valley.

"Is everybody ready to play?" my dad asked. He then turned his back to us and shouted, "Green light!"

We tiptoed toward him from twenty feet away, freezing in mid-step whenever he whirled around and yelled, "Red light!" One time he caught us all in motion. "Back back back, all of you! Back to the beginning." Rufi remained frozen in case my dad had missed her. "You, too, young lady," he said, spinning her around by the shoulders and spanking her back to the starting line. "Get on back. Get on back where you belong and just try to fool this old fox."

We couldn't, especially because of his face. Whenever he did twirl around and we were motionless, he would come up to us in our odd, frozen positions and make contorted faces at us. He'd bulge his eyes and twist his nose and waggle his tongue out at us. We'd laugh, Rufi most of all, and my dad would push us backwards, saying, "Back to your cages, all of you. All you monkeys back where you belong."

My dad was alive, as alive as I'd ever seen him. There probably wasn't much difference between him now and him in 1925 on East 61st and Superior, playing this same game in the same dusk-light with a mother inside preparing dinner. Now, sixty-five years later, he laughed himself to tears when Cindy finally outsmarted him and won. And I thought: Dad, it sure took you a long time to become young.

The light in the sky had faded enough for us to see lantern light up and down the valley. We could dimly see coils of smoke rising from all the kitchens. Domestic work was being done out there and inside this house, but not by us. Our work was to play. From red light, green light and now to hide-'n-go-seek, we five children kept running in our golden immortal hillside time.

We hid while Rufi counted. With her head against the porch post she counted to one hundred in English, skipping most of the numbers and peeking out at us from the edges of her fists. Cindy and Lakshmi knelt behind a coconut tree. I climbed a mango tree, pausing to notice a charred nook in the trunk that held a candle and a small chipped statue of Buddha. My dad hid in the open. In a flash of either brilliance or insanity, he stood out in a clearing with his arms raised and twisted like a tree. I watched a trail of ants near my hands, and then I watched Rufi, done counting, walk *right past* my father.

Suddenly he broke from his pose. "Yeeeeeeeeeiooowwww!" he howled, and ran toward the goal of the porch post. His was not a run but a stagger, my ancient father lurching along as stiffly as if on stilts. He howled again and Rufi gave chase. I wished from my perch in the mango tree that this scene would never end, a scene of a little girl forever reaching and an old father forever in motion, forever ahead.

But she caught him, easily, and together they fell down laughing. That was sweet music, that laughter. Sacred music, really, and I wished that it could roll down the hillside and roll over all the soldiers and gem dealers and drunken Jewel, healing them all. The healing would come through connections, like this least likely of all connections standing before me: Rufi and the judge. Despite their separate origins—my father from the cold of inner-city Cleveland, a world of brick and gray and drifting snow; Rufi from the steaming jungle, a world of vines and green and monsoon rains—despite all of that they somehow managed to drop their differences and connect on the field of play.

The front door opened. *Dinner in ten minutes,* Sarala announced. *But first, puja.*

Rufi whined at this nightly call to prayer. *I want to play with Sudu Tattaaaaaaaaaaaaa,* she complained, and then, seeing flowers and a lit candle in her mother's hands, she sprinted across the yard to her, hopping across a hopscotch grid along the way. Sarala handed her the flowers and together they laid their offerings in the nook of the mango tree. The candle illuminated the statue of Buddha, its left arm and chin chipped off, its surface covered in soot, its eyes positioned at odd angles. Sarala bowed before the statue and then retreated into the house, hiding behind a shutter. My father asked Cindy why she was doing that.

"Must be having her period," Cindy said. "They believe that a woman who's menstruating is too unclean to worship in a puja."

My dad and I, always uneasy around female business, nodded with great maturity and said nothing. He then folded himself like the rest of us into a cross-legged position on the ground. "Jimmy," he said, "I'll need the fire department to get me out of this pretzel."

Yaseratne led the *puja* prayers in the ancient, sacred language of Sanskrit. For the first half of each prayer he spoke alone, followed by a chorus from the rest of us. Lakshmi took all of this very seriously; Rufi, meanwhile, was more preoccupied with all the ways she could interlace her fingers. As for me, though I understood none of the prayers, I could feel the mystery and reverence in the rhythms of the language, similar to how I always felt hearing Latin in a Catholic service. But more than the Sanskrit, it was the Buddha statue that I loved the most. Cross-eyed and charred, it was holier to me in its damaged state than anything in any golden-roofed temple.

Afterwards we ate. All seven of us crowded into the dark, smoky kitchen lit only by the fire, squatting on low benches with our knees jutting up high. My father, pleased there were no cane chairs in sight, needed my help getting down. Yaseratne recited a Buddhist prayer, then asked my father if he wanted to say his Christian grace.

"Keep it short, Dad," I said.

He folded his hands. "Thank you, Lord, for the life in this house and for the food on my plate. Amen."

I looked over at him in disbelief. "Dad, I didn't mean—"

"I'm hungry," he said. "Let's do some damage."

And so we ate. Rufi, pretending she was a giant and the rice kernels were people, mashed up whole families and villages with an ogre's growl and gulped them down. When she tired of that massacre she played with the hairs on my toes, looking up now and then to laugh at my dad's struggle with the finger routine. His rice was flying everywhere. Yaseratne, after getting hit in the eye by a rice missile, leaned over to adjust the angle of my father's thumb. It worked, and from then on the balls of curry and rice flew intact into my dad's mouth.

"Got the knack of it now," my dad boasted. "Oh, wait'll Lil sees this!"

Later that night my dad distributed some gifts. The Lemon Twist baffled the girls, its bells and computer-operated counter too alien to children accustomed to gifts of buttons and glue. I knew the fate of the Lemon Twist: Too valuable to ever be played with, it would sit protected in its cellophane wrapping behind a glass case. But the family put all the other gifts to immediate use: Yaseratne modeled his Ohio State Buckeyes T-shirt for us; Sarala wanted to plant her vegetable seeds right then in the darkness; Rufi invented her own rules for pick-up-sticks; and Lakshmi, intent as an engraver, colored in Garfield with some of the crayons from her box of 164 Crayolas. They continued this after my father said good-night and went to bed. In a few minutes he called me into the bedroom.

"What are those, Jimmy?" he asked.

I looked up on the walls. "Those? Oh, don't worry, they're just geckos, and they just go for mosquitoes. They'll stay stuck to the wall, but if they fall off it's good luck. Boy, there sure are a lot of them tonight."

"And what about that, and all those?"

He was pointing to the cockroaches. These were not your ordinary Cleveland cockroaches, but more like something from the mind of a science-fiction animator: three inches of black body, three inches of waving antennae, scuttling, scratching, and, worst of all, flying. I told my dad about my first night in Sri Lanka. One of these monsters flew between my glasses and my eye, lodging there, its wings battering frantically and its antennae scraping my forehead. "I was ready to turn around and return home right then. Compared to me, Dad, you're doing great."

He knelt down beside the bed. "Well, if that goat didn't kill me, I don't suppose these little critters can do me in. Anyhow, good night, Jimmy. I'm just going to say the rosary and call it a night."

"Good night, Dad."

I turned to leave. At the doorway I paused to watch him leaning heavily over the bed on his elbows, fingering his rosary beads. I was surprised at my impulse to join him. The rosary had always annoyed me as a kid. He'd drag out those beads on family vacations, in the car, even on the back porch with my friends on summer nights. Its only appeal to me was the sound of the words, like "blessed bosom of Jesus," which for a while I thought meant that Jesus, like most of my Irish relatives, was fond of booze.

Thirty years later I found cause to kneel down beside him. There amid the geckos and the cockroaches I prayed knee-to-knee with my father. I didn't want to be anywhere else. While praying I realized that the rosary is just like the Buddhist *puja*: the same repetition of a prayer, the same alternation of solo and chorus, the same idea of a body position that keeps the mind alert.

When we finished he put his hand on mine and thanked me. I helped him into bed, flicking aside a cockroach on his pillow that I hoped he hadn't seen. I unfurled the mosquito net over him and dimmed the kerosene lantern and again wished him good-night.

I watched him fall asleep. There were noises outside the room—pick-up sticks, the sharpening of a crayon, Arrow barking, distant explosions—but all that mattered was the sound of my father snoring. I stood over him and watched through the netting the rising of his chest and the movement of his jaw, the swallowing, the jerking, the scratching. I sat down for a closer look. He has tiny warts on his eyelids. The inside of his ears are pretty clean. He misses a lot of spots while shaving. He has a tiny scar on his chin that I'll have to ask him about.

I felt that my eyes were still too far away. Quietly so as not to wake him, I lifted the mosquito net as if lifting a bridal veil and lowered my head to meet his head. I paused to observe the topography of his skin, and then lowered myself some more until I did what I hadn't done for a long, long time, maybe forever: I kissed my dad on his forehead.

This man is my father. I could feel the weight of that truth settle inside me, and with it I could feel a connection to every son from every age. This man is my father.

I had no idea what any of this was all about. All I really knew as I stood up to leave, quietly tucking the mosquito netting into the edges of the bed, was that it felt like I had been in that room for many days.

The next morning at dawn we cut rice.

It was men's work. We walked at dawn along the narrow hillside path down to the fields. Yaseratne led the way with three long and narrow tree trunks balanced on his head, my father and I behind carrying sickles and a tall thermos of tea. Other groups of men joined us on the path. Each man owned a few acres of arable land, distributed in 1948 when the British ended their rule. This wide availability of food helped to make Sri Lanka a relatively healthy country, with a long life expectancy (around seventy) and a low infant-mortality rate.

On the walk to the rice field we passed the white, bell-shaped Buddhist temple that most of these men had helped to build. One of the men had painted the images of Buddha inside; when painting the eyes, he had followed the Buddhist practice of turning away from the image and using a mirror. He and the others now stopped to tie ribbons onto the branches of a bo tree out front—a bo tree, as the story goes, from the original bo tree that Buddha had sat under in northern India. Their ribbons represented prayers, which on this day concerned the rice harvest. They prayed a little longer, tidied up the grounds, and then returned to the path. While walking I asked Yaseratne for an update on the war situation in his village.

*It's still quiet, he said, but things are changing. Last month the JVP soldiers came to our house twice. They wear ski masks and hold guns, and for the rest of the night the girls cry and cannot sleep. They just want money now, but who knows about tomorrow. Jayara, the principal, he was killed. Two bus drivers from the village—both killed. We live with tragedy in this country. But I also have good news.*

*What's that?*

*Soon, maybe next month, electricity will come to our village. Oh, Jim, soon we can watch television.*

I told him to be careful, that in some ways a culture had more to fear from a television set than from an entire JVP army. I had already seen the damage in a few families. In one case, we used to eat dinner with a family huddled in a tight circle around candles, discussing and joking, and afterwards would invent silly games; that all changed with the arrival of the TV, which was left on at dinner-time and killed all talk, killed all invention. From one day to the next I had seen lively faces become zombies, and I feared this fate for Yaseratne's family. When I told him that television is the world's most intoxicating drug, he laughed and said I was exaggerating as usual.

Down at the rice field a group of other farmers were waiting for us. Two of them had grotesquely enlarged goiters supported by cloth slings around their necks. Every time I had seen one of these goiters—and they were a common sight in Sri Lanka—I recalled the "Goiter Fund" my friends and I kept in third grade. For some reason we were terrified of waking up one day with one of these melons hanging from our throats, so with the nickels in our "Goiter Fund" we bought iodized salt and ate it straight.

None of the farmers had a full set of teeth, which became apparent when they smiled at this alien sight of an old white American man come to cut their rice. My dad bowed to each of them and said, "Ayubowan."

One of the goiter men exclaimed, *Sinhala! He speaks Sinhala! Yasie, you cannot have this honored man—he speaks Sinhala!—you cannot have him cut our rice. He cannot be our servant. Sinhala!*

Yaseratne tucked his Ohio State Buckeyes T-shirt into his sarong. *He insists. I tell him to sleep and eat but no. He wants to come and work. We must obey him.*

After translating this to my dad he replied, "Tell them, Jimmy, that I just don't want to slow these good folks down. They have work to do and I just appreciate being out here and seeing rice. Ate this stuff my whole life and never been up close to it."

All the farmers agreed that if my dad went slowly, it would be a good thing. *You can teach us like the Buddha*, one of them said. *Teach us to go slow and to be present.* He then handed my dad his sickle. *This is the oldest sickle in the village, sir, and still the best. My great-grandfather, he made with his own hands. You bless me by using it today.*

My dad stared at the sickle, feeling the weight of history in its uneven steel, and said, "Well, thank you. I'm not sure how to work one of these but, Jimmy, you tell these folks that I sure feel honored and I'll sure try my best."

We eight men stood in a straight line facing the rising sun. Following Yaseratne's lead, we raised our sickles above our heads and bowed as he said, *To the sun and the rain and the gods who give us our rice, we offer our thanks and our work.* We passed the sickles three times around our backs, raised them back up to the sun, and then went to work.

Yaseratne, being the eldest, cut the first handful of rice shafts. He prayed during the cutting, and prayed again while sprinkling the first rice kernels back into the earth. I joked to my dad that we should have done all this praying when we scooped the wet leaves and pigeon crap out of the gutters each spring. "Can you imagine us holding the trowels up to the sun?"

My dad gave this some thought. "You know, Jimmy, that might not have been such a bad idea."

The eight of us lined up in a row and worked, bent over at the waist, slicing handfuls of rice and dropping them behind us. We worked around the scarecrows of coconut branches arranged to look like cobras. We moved as a unit, though my father tended to cut a little too quickly and move ahead of the row.

*Slow down, sir,* Yaseratne said. *We must cut slowly and steadily like the Buddha says, like a water buffalo that moves itself out of the mud. No hurry. You must give all of yourself to every blade you cut. The Buddha tells us this. Now repeat after me: "Teeka teeka."* This expression, meaning "little by little I can," was heard every hour in every situation in Sri Lanka, almost like a national motto. *"Teeka teeka,"* sir, *and everything will get done.*

"Teeka teeka," my dad responded, wobbling his head like Yaseratne, and little by little the eight of us moved in a line through the field with the morning sun heating our backs. This harvest had special meaning to me. The very blades I cut were from the seed I had planted three months earlier, standing calf-deep in muddy water. This harvest completed the first of the year's three rice harvests, though the farmers feared that a foreign invader was gradually reducing that number to two. The invader was the pine forest, now looming across the hilltops like a cavalry ready to charge. The pine tree was spreading throughout Sri Lanka courtesy of the World Bank, which had loaned money to Sri Lanka on the condition that they import the Bank's ideas to stop hillside erosion. In came the pine and eucalyptus trees, trees that grow fast and indeed hold the soil but suck up water like no other tree. Their thirst disturbs the water table, reducing the amount of water available in this valley to grow rice. Three harvests were becoming two harvests, and even those two had new problems from the pine forest. The acidity from the fallen pine needles was killing many indigenous plants on the forest floor, upsetting the ecosystem of bugs and predators surrounding the rice fields. For all these reasons the farm families of Sri Lanka referred to the pine tree, which in America is considered fragrant, as *ganga*—that is, as "shit."

But for now at the rice field we were just men at work. By the time the sun was directly overhead we eight men had cleared Yaseratne's field, and another neighbor's, and another's, stopping often for tea and for a chew of betel. My father asked whose fields were whose but in fact there were no clear lines. There were no clear lines between any of this—between field and field, work and rest, work and vacation, work-week and weekend, work-life and retirement. At my mention of a weekend in America, they would ask, *Weekend? Please explain this idea of a weekend.* The clear American division between work-time and fun-time does not exist in Sri Lanka. For them, the relaxation of an American weekend is woven into their work. What then appears as a slow, lazy way of working—and this applies to teachers, bankers, politicians, as well as farmers—is really a spiritual way of working.

By noon the women had arrived at the rice field. Sarala and Lakshmi carried our lunches on their heads, Cindy carried burlap bags and a sheet, and Rufi pretended to be a lion pouncing on the cobra scarecrows. Before eating, we hoisted piles of the newly cut rice shafts onto the burlap sacks and then onto our heads, carrying them like outlandish bonnets. We dropped our loads in a circular area that had been stamped down to level dirt. There the stack grew, and when all the rice had been moved to it, we seven collapsed down onto it. We ate our lunch of rice and curry (always rice and curry) from banana-leaf plates. Surrounding us in every direction were the stepped terraces of rice fields, forming a colossal amphitheater with us on center stage. We lay back and admired the color and symmetry of the landscape, the six of us in sarongs and one in wool pants. The wool-panted guy breathed deeply and closed his eyes, but never fell asleep. From his smile I could tell he knew that Rufi was inserting spikes of rice straw in his hair.

There arrived a pair of water buffalo belonging to the neighbor. This was the farmers' threshing machine, these two mammoth, docile animals yoked together at the neck, their horns wide and twisted. We rose from the bed of rice. Yaseratne, blessing the buffalo, led them onto the stack that still held the imprint of our bodies. He steered the buffalo around and around in a tight circle, whipping their hides with a stick and shouting, "Heeyaa!"

I explained to my dad that the friction of the hooves breaks off the kernels, which then work their way through the straw down to the ground. "Later we'll move the straw away and there it'll all be, the rice all ready to be swept up."

"Amazing," my dad said. "And not an engine in sight."

For the next four hours we worked this procedure in two teams of three—Yaseratne with Sarala and Lakshmi, Cindy with my dad and me—while Rufi was off imprisoning frogs in a stream with her pick-up sticks. For our team, my dad steered the buffalo around in a circle, shouting "Heeyaa!" with great gusto and seriousness. Cindy turned the straw over with a pitchfork, while I, for some reason, got the enviable job of trailing the animals' rumps with a handful of straw to catch their frequent plops.

On this day I loved Plop Patrol. I loved this entire time-warped scene, three twentieth-century white Americans at work crushing rice in the exact way with the exact tools on the exact spot as a tenth-century Sri Lankan. My dad ran his hand along the hide of the outside buffalo, which he had named "Lil," feeling its horns and its ears and looking closely into its eyes. "Heeyaa, Lil!" he'd yell.

An hour before sunset the wind kicked up. The farmers expected this, of course, since they seemed to anticipate every shift of nature. It would rain tomorrow—Yaseratne sniffed the air to determine this—and then it would rain every day after that for the next month.

The monsoon season was here. This news concerned me because the rains might prevent my dad and me from swimming in the ocean. The news concerned Yaseratne because in order to save his crop, we had to finish the harvest tonight.

For the final stage, the cleaning of the rice, Yaseratne began by leaning the three narrow tree trunks against each other to form a tripod. Then, blessing the trees and his knees, he put his foot into Sarala's interlocked fingers and climbed onto the intersecting joint. In front of the tripod Sarala placed a sheet, which she blessed, while Cindy and I pushed aside the trampled straw to get to the rice kernels. We gathered the kernels, along with dirt and twigs, in bowls that we handed up to Yaseratne in his perch. He watched the horizon like a sailor sighting land, sniffing the air, turning his ear into the setting sun. Then, before any of us could feel anything, Yaseratne threw a bowlful of dirty rice into the air that the wind, gusting at that exact moment, caught in midair. The dirt, the pebbles, the twigs, the rice—each fell according to its weight in distinct areas on the sheet. All of us except Rufi, who was off riding "Lil," swept away the unwanted particles, leaving only rice on the sheet which we emptied into a gunny sack.

"It's ingenious," my dad said. "Wind and gravity and that's all you need. My oh my, Malone would sure be singing a different tune about this place if he could see this operation."

We repeated the procedure over and over with each bowlful, finishing at the exact moment the wind died down for the night. Yaseratne climbed down off the tripod and, facing the half-set sun, held up a small handful of rice. We all did, and we all passed the rice three times around our backs before throwing the kernels out into the darkness and back into the earth.

The rains came the next afternoon, and for every afternoon that followed. In the mornings we played under clear blue skies and later under shadows of clouds, and by afternoon the first heavy drops of rain pushed us inside. Between four and five o'clock we could barely talk over the rain. Before dinner the mist turned to fog; after dinner the fog turned to clear, starlit nights. And each night before going to bed we stood outside looking up at the sky.

Our days passed in play. Rufi's favorite was riding on my dad's back while he was down on all fours, pretending he was a buffalo and calling him "Lil." She would yoke him to me using a ribbon, then steer us big white men over some rice straw that Sarala had spread out for us on the living-room floor. Lakshmi would look up from her coloring book, laugh, then return to experimenting with all 164 colors in her Crayola box. I noticed that she had taped the Sinhala word for each color on the barrel of each crayon. And I noticed that the Lemon Twist, still in plastic and still unopened, remained behind the glass case. A Frisbee leaned against it.

Yaseratne was so amazed at another of our games that he brought home a new group of friends every night to play it. The game was the childhood slumber-party trick of "light as a feather," in which four people lifted a seated person above their heads with just their interlocked fingers, all done with incantations, all very spooky. The trick astonished these Sri Lankans. Every night more and more people came to the house, each insisting on being lifted by the three white magicians and Rufi. "Light as fetta, light as fetta," the crowd in the room would chant, and when we lifted the person up high, the house would erupt in cheers. By the third night Rufi wore a wizard's starry hat and waved a pick-up-stick as her magic wand.

But the true magic came every night when we stared up at the stars. My dad marveled at seeing more stars than he ever thought existed. Yaseratne seemed to know every constellation and every story behind every one of them. My dad didn't know a thing, which is why it surprised me when he pointed to one insignificant light and said, "Now that one. That's gotta be Saturn."

Yaseratne confirmed that indeed it was Saturn, spoken casually as if it were no big deal to pull Saturn out of a crowded sky. I asked my dad how a guy from Cleveland could possibly identify Saturn.

He said that he had seen it once as a child through a telescope with his father, and that it had stayed with him. "Every time I look up at it, I think of him. I think of him taking me—just me, Jimmy—out to the observatory over at Case University. You know, we were just poor city people, and here one day my dad says in his Irish brogue, 'Johnny, how's about you and me be seein' Saturn tonight?'

"Well, I was thrilled. I was just a little kid, and any time I could be alone with my dad—we had nine sisters, remember, and just two bedrooms for the lot of us—any time alone with him was a thrill to me. So we ride the streetcar out to Case, and it's cold. Lots of snow on the ground, clear sky. He sits on the edge of the bench, my dad, and he's so excited he tells a strange lady, 'Me son and me, we're goin' to see Saturn. Imagine that, will ya? Saturn!'

"So we walk up the steps to the telescope. It's cold in there, so cold you could see your breath, and all these adults let me come up front. My dad, he picks me up by the waist, he puts my eye to the eyepiece and he says, 'Johnny, I give you Saturn.' I'll never forget it, Jimmy. I *saw* the rings. It was a little fuzzy but by God I could *see* the rings of Saturn. And my dad, he's standing over me with a smile like I've never seen on him. When I'm done it's his turn, and he looks. Probably the first time in his entire life the guy has looked above the telephone wires. So he looks—I'll never forget it, Jimmy—and while he's looking he says, 'Ahhhhh.' Over and over again just like that: 'Ahhhhh.'

"Back home he tucks me into bed. A first for him. He tucks me in and says to me real serious, 'Johnny, don't you be forgettin' to look up now.' I must've stared up at him like *he* was Saturn. Then he kisses my cheek and again he says real quiet, 'Never forget it, Johnny. Never forget to look up.'"

On our last night we watched the full moon. Lakshmi leaned against the mango tree, drawing the night sky on a paper sack with her crayons. Above her head was the tree's nook, and I could see by the light of the *puja* candle that the chipped statue of Buddha was missing. I turned to ask Rufi about this but she was too busy riding a broom around the yard, waving her wizard's hat, saying over and over, "I light as fetta . . . whooosh! I light as fetta . . . whoosh!" Suddenly she dropped both broom and hat and jumped on top of my dad's back.

*Sudu Tatta,* she said, pointing to the moon, *look at the rabbit. The rabbit in the moon!*

My dad searched but could find nothing. "Nope, no rabbit. Now the man in the moon, him I can see. The eyes, the mouth. You see, Rufi?"

She said there was only room on the moon for a rabbit and that no rabbit would ever share a moon with a man. She climbed higher on his back and tilted his head. *There, the ears. And there, a little nose. That's a rabbit nose, and this*—she honked my dad's big nose—*is a Sudu Tatta nose.*

In time my dad found the rabbit, Rufi found the man, and while Rufi darted from person to person pointing out her new discovery—*it's obvious, Lakshmi!*—my dad walked over to me. "A whole lifetime, Jimmy, a whole lifetime I look at the moon and, whadya know, I never see a rabbit. A rabbit, right under my nose! Wait'll I show this to Lil. Just imagine: a rabbit! Jimmy, can you see the rabbit up there?"

I barely heard him. I had arched my neck in another direction and, seeing the Big Dipper, immediately felt the chemistry of my body change. The Big Dipper still owned me. It had now been a year since our bus accident, a year since the brakes failed that wet night coming down the steep mountain road, and still the Big

Dipper owned me. It had been a year since I saw in Cindy's wild eyes and felt in her wild grip that, yes, this careening moment in a runaway bus was indeed the moment of our death. My last earthly emotion became clear to me: grieving for my parents that would bury their baby Jimmy, and grieving for my brother Joe, wandering the gray streets of Cleveland in sorrow. Then the crash, the bodies colliding off each other like dolls, the screech of rending metal and the ceiling become the floor. Then it all stopped. I untwisted myself and crawled from the wreckage with Cindy to the roadside. We curled up and rocked, sobbing so heavily from the nearness of death that I wondered what black spring could endlessly feed my tears. Then through those tears I looked up at the sky and saw the most beautiful sight I'd ever seen. It was the Big Dipper. Its quiet beauty silenced all earthly sounds—the sobs, the cries of agony from the survivors, the sirens—and I felt its seven stars reach down and raise me in its ladle to sit in heaven among all the pearls. Maybe for five seconds, maybe for five years, I rocked on the ladle of the Big Dipper as if in a great mother's arms, rocked and soothed by lullabies that whispered this truth in my ear: You are alive, Jimmy. By a random throw of the dice, you are alive. The driver plunged the bus into a house to save you, killing himself but saving you. A stranger died for you. A stranger died and others died but you are alive, still alive to weep at the simple, silent beauty of the Big Dipper. There it is, now and always, the eternal fire of those seven sparkling pearls reminding you of the majesty and the mystery of life. Just remember one thing: Don't forget to look up, Jimmy. Don't ever forget to look up.

My dad was asking again if I could see the rabbit in the moon. I thought of telling him about the bus crash, but I sensed too strongly that a holy event like that would become melodrama and gossip here on earth. So instead I just linked my arm through his and pulled him close, feeling the deeper love that comes from mortality. And I wondered: Does he love me less because I am the son, the one who thinks he will live on and on? For fathers are the dying ones, children are the immortal ones, but what is it that gets lost in the loving when a father thinks his son will never die?

"Oh, she's easy to see, Jimmy. You see at two o'clock, those are the ears, and over there at eight is her little tail. It's a puffy little tail."

"Yeah, yeah. I see her, Dad," I said, pulling him closer. "I see it all."

I felt a stick tapping the back of my head and turned around. *Pretzel! I command you to play pretzel!* It was Rufi, tapping me on the head with her magic wand. *Come follow Queen Rufi and come play pretzel."* She went from head to head repeating this until all of us were gathered in a circle in the center of the yard. Rufi waved her wand around us and chanted, *Pretzel, pretzel, in the night . . .*

We created a human pretzel, holding hands with two different people across the circle. We then tried to unravel this tangle without breaking hands, but from the start each of our moves seemed to complicate the pretzel. It appeared insolvable until my dad (he of the legal mind) took over.

"Jimmy, you put your leg through there . . . no, no, over *there!* That's it, and Queen Rufi, you go under Cindy's legs. Yaseratne, over Sarala, and Lakshmi, Lakshmi, . . . What am I going to do about Lakshmi?" He thought for a moment. "Here, you go through my arms. That's it, that's it, you got it . . ."

Soon he had it all unraveled, the seven of us holding hands in a circle lit by the spotlight of a full moon. On my right side I held my father's soft hand, and on my left I held Yaseratne's, a rough and thick hand that knew hard work. Yaseratne released my grip and stepped into the center of the circle. He gently pulled my dad in with him, saying, *Please, sir, my family has something for you. A gift. A simple gift from simple people.*

In that moment in that circle beneath the rabbit and the Big Dipper, Yaseratne placed something in my dad's palm that made me ache with joy. He closed my father's fingers over the gift, and he said,

*You give us so much, sir. You cut our rice, you play with my children. My girls, my girls love you very much. There is no gift I can give you like that. I am very sorry.* Rufi pried open my dad's fingers and pulled down his palm to her eye level. I knew from the expression on her face that my father now held a gift more valuable than any sapphire or any golden tooth in any golden temple. He stared at the gift for a long time, saying over and over, "Ahhhhh." Just like that, "Ahhhhh," as if it were Saturn in the palm of his hand, as if it were the Big Dipper in the palm of his hand. He then slowly closed his fingers back over it and slid it into the pocket of his wool pants to rest alongside his rosary.

He pulled his empty hand out of his pocket, and I could see that his fingertips still held some ash from rubbing against the chipped and sooty Buddha.

9

And then it was time to go home, to my ragged Bandarawela home.

A month earlier this had me worried—my dad scoffing at the mud floors and the twig walls and the outhouse, scoffing at the Buddha shrine, scoffing at the flat rock on which we washed our clothes. I was even more worried that while observing me teach, he would glance at his watch and kill me with a yawn. He'd never utter it, but somewhere in his smirk he'd be saying to me, "Jimmy, teaching is sweet but oh boy how I could've set you up in the law. Could've set you up with some top-flight law firm or got you on the bench in no time. My robe, it could've been yours, all of it yours, if only . . . well, if only you'd answered that question right. *Yellow Cab v The State of New York*, I'm surprised that one stumped you."

But those worries were now gone. No man with a chipped Buddha in his pocket could smirk in that way. He sat across from me on the train from Kandy to Bandarawela, making funny taffy faces to a baby. No one who makes faces like that could really care about a son blanking out in a law class. He now knew in his fingers the feel of a water buffalo's hide, and his shoulders now knew the weight of Rufi, all drenched and muddy. There's a rabbit in the moon—this he now knew—and there's plenty of room on a forehead for a dab of saffron dust. Put it all together, and I knew that this father sitting across from me was no longer the slaying kind.

He was more of the *wadee* kind. "Jimmy, see if you can rustle us up a wadee or two," and I did and we ate a coneful with tea. When the conductor came for our money, my dad gave him three *wadee*s and ninety cents. That was the entire fare, ninety cents for a six-hour train journey for three people. I tried to pay but my dad insisted. "It'll set me back a bit but, hey, no sense going to the grave with an extra ninety cents rattling around your pocket."

Our attention alternated between the lush jungle scenery outside and the singers inside, seated on the floor in a circle near the door. They were a group of young men singing the same twenty-minute songs their ancestors had sung to pass the time on long journeys. While they sang, many others in the train clapped or beat makeshift drums. My dad did, too, clapping the baby's hands next to him. So engrossed was he that it took him a few extra seconds to notice that everyone else had suddenly fallen silent. Among the singing men there were whispers and a flurry of activity, and then one of the men in a turban stood and swiftly disappeared out the door of the moving train. The silence grew deeper.

Two soldiers entered the car. They were in no hurry, and on their agonizing saunter down the aisle they were far too polite—tipping their helmets to old men, tickling babies, letting small boys touch their rifles. When they arrived at the circle of men on the floor, the tension thickened in the train. No one spoke and no one locked eyes, and I wondered if anyone on the train was even breathing. One of the soldiers asked the men something. When there was no answer the soldier sucked deep on his cigarette and asked again, this time with his rifle tickling a man's neck. The train wheels squealed against the tight rails. The soldier asked again and again, his rifle driven deeper into the neck, and then—such is the insanity of Sri Lankan life—laughed wildly and walked away, motioning the other soldier to follow.

An old woman across from me watched their exit very intently. When the soldiers were far gone she looped out the window a strip of fabric with a stone tied to the end. She held it there for a minute and then reeled it back in. I soon understood that this was a signal given to someone hiding beneath the train. The someone, now returning through the door, was the turbaned man who had fled the soldiers a little earlier. Panting, his clothes tattered and dirt red, he leaned heavily onto his friends for support, his eyes wide with shock—the shock that comes from hanging on for dear life to the underside of a train.

It took a while for the singing to resume. After one song in which no one remembered the words, and then another without any spirit, the songs picked up in volume and in clapping. After a few songs one of the older men, having noticed my dad's tapping foot, approached us and asked a question. I translated it to my dad.

"He wants you to sing an American song," I said. "A solo."

"Me? Out loud? Oh, good God, Jimmy, they'll jump off the train when they hear my voice."

"Oh, c'mon, be a sport. Just pretend you're Sinatra at Vegas."

"No, no, no. Old Blue Eyes I certainly am not."

I explained to him that one of the beauties of Sri Lankan culture is that ridicule doesn't exist. "Sing anything, Dad, and they'll love it. They won't have a clue what you're singing and they'll love it anyhow."

"Nope. You go tell them that old Frank has laryngitis."

I didn't press him on this one. Singing embarrassed me, too, so during my first year in Sri Lanka I declined all offers to sing—and an oddity of the culture is that they ask it all the time. I feared being ridiculed, and I maintained that fear until I eventually realized that glorious trait of Sri Lanka: People *never* ridicule anybody. They never ridicule the fat boy or the girl with acne, never ridicule the slow learner or the disabled. And above all they never ridicule the singer, even if all the dogs in the neighborhood are howling.

This emboldened me. I started off slow but by my second year I was a singing fool. When asked to sing I stood up tall, belting out songs with a robustness that startled birds out of trees. I was ridicule-free! I sang when asked and sang when not asked. I was an Elvis movie come to life, me breaking out into song in train stations and in restaurants. At first I sang Peace Corps cliches—"Blowin' in the Wind," "Puff, The Magic Dragon," "Where Have All the Flowers Gone"—until I realized that I wasn't a nun and could sing anything at all: "Satisfaction," "Proud Mary," my high-school fight song, even "Timothy," a 1960s tune about marooned friends eating Timothy. The Sri Lankans understood nothing and swayed to everything.

Here on the train to Bandarawela when they asked me to sing, I chose "American Pie," a song as endless as some of theirs. I remembered a few words and just invented the rest:

> Oh, for ten years we've been on our own,
> And moss covers my kidney stones,
> But that's not how it uuuuuuuuuuuuuused to be.

It went on like that for ten minutes, the crowd swaying and clapping and tossing me *wadees* like coins. My dad shrunk into the corner of his seat, and farther still when Cindy began to sing Led Zeppelin's "Stairway to Heaven," complete with improvised lines like the last one, "And we're buying an AMC Gremlin." When finished, she made a very flamboyant bow and caught *wadees* in midair. My dad smiled and shook his head, twirling his finger around his ear in the universal language that said, "The two of you are out of your minds."

From the Bandarawela train station we walked downhill to our home. Word had already spread that "Jimge Tatta" had arrived from America, and with that news came activity. From all the houses overlooking the road we heard shouts of "Ayubowan, Jimge Tatta!"

and invitations for tea. As we passed the dusty cricket field, the players stopped their game to welcome my dad to Bandarawela. Farther down the road a little girl ran from her home to present us with three mangoes, calling, "Ayubowan, Jimge Tatta!"

The owner of a tiny *kadee* emerged from his dark tin shack, sidestepping a cardboard Kodak model with her bathing suit peeled away. "Ayubowan, Jimge Tatta," he bowed, then rose and offered us a stalk of bananas.

We accepted, and then we heard the loudest greeting of all. It came from Nishanka, a fifteen-year-old girl banished indoors for life because she was mute. She rattled her bedroom shutter to get our attention and then, with her body hidden in the shadows, welcomed us by patting the air with her fingers. The shout of mute Nishanka.

To all these people my dad was a deity. A bizarre deity, true, with his white Totes umbrella and Gatorade bottle, but a deity nonetheless. Part of that stature came from his being associated with me, the teacher. But even more came just by being old, being white, and being a visitor from afar. The eminent people in Sri Lankan culture are not the millionaire investment bankers or game-show hosts or professional athletes. Instead, respect goes out to the elderly and to the teachers, to monks and to mothers, to small children and to guests.

This day we Americans were on parade. For the entire mile's walk we never stopped waving, an action that soon fatigued me. But not my dad. He was an old hand at this parade business, having walked in the last fifty St. Patrick's Day parades in Cleveland. He knew how to wave his hand mechanically, how to freeze his smile, how to turn his face up at just the right angle—all done while sidestepping mounds of horse shit in Cleveland and elephant shit in Bandarawela.

"Oh, Jimmy, this here is the life," he sighed, waving to the steady line of Sri Lankans. "Look at all these people greeting us, all these smiles! Oh, what I'd give to have Malone see these folks rolling out the red carpet like this."

Farther down the road two little girls dangled upside-down from the branch of a mango tree, their skirts turned inside-out around their faces. They raised their skirts to see my dad, who had turned his own head upside-down to look back at the girls. He made one goofy clown face at them and then another. They giggled so hard that they coughed for breath.

My dad asked me about the problem with their eyes. Both girls had an eye that wandered on its own, a condition we had called "lazy eye" in my grade school. I envied those classmates who had it. The nuns permitted them to wear a patch in school over the good eye, pirate-like, to build the muscles of the "lazy eye." But these girls in the mango tree would get no patches and no medical attention, creating vision problems for the rest of their lives.

My dad shook his head. "Can't something be done for them? Can't you just rig up a rubber band and a piece of paper?" He paused just long enough for me to wonder why I had no answer. "I tell you, Jimmy, when I get back to Cleveland I'll be having a good long talk with Dr. Koster, see if we can't rustle something on up to send over here. As for those damn saxophones, well, maybe they'll just have to wait."

We walked on, surrounded by more invitations for tea, more waves and more *ayubowan*s and more gifts of fruit. A cow strolled past us without any owner in sight, its hooves clicking like high heels on the asphalt. For a moment it stopped to stare at us with its vacant, milky eyes until my father, staring back, began to moo. The cow tilted its head to make sense of this madman. Nearby, the girls in the mango tree giggled and swayed.

An old barefoot man with a purple turban limped up the road toward us. He smacked the cow with his cane for no apparent reason. Then, unfazed that we were only two feet away, he closed one nostril and snorted a stream of snot onto the ground. He looked at it, appeared satisfied, then hobbled away.

To my surprise, my dad thought this nose trick rather nifty and worth learning. He clamped a nostril shut with one finger and asked, "Is this it, Jimmy? Just one side like this?"

I manipulated my dad's fingers on his nose as if it were a clarinet. (I wondered: How did I get to be the expert in this field?) I instructed him to "lean forward and snort quick and clean." He did, mastering it on the very first snort.

"Hey hey hey hey hey," he marveled. "That's nice. That's clean. Kids, I see a bright future in this."

"No time to gloat," Cindy said, pointing up the road. "Not when the queen is paying a visit."

The queen was Amma, our landlord and neighbor, running barefoot toward us while flashing a one-toothed smile. For her to run at all was quite a feat. Obese and sixty-five, Amma's body swayed so much from the swing of her huge breasts that, at a trot, she had the solid, oscillating motion of a boat in heavy seas.

Amma, dear sweet old toothless Amma, was a thief. Though rich by Sri Lankan standards, she stole from us nonetheless: pens, a few plates, two cassettes (Aretha Franklin and U2), a coconut, a pillow. She stole my *Offensive Schemes of the Boston Celtics*. She stole my high-top Nikes for a week; I found them returned on my doorstep, stretched beyond use by her broad feet. Once Cindy caught her red-handed, heisting a cheap brass ornament off our wall. When Amma raised her arms innocently, the ornament fell from her armpit and clattered on the floor. With a bewildered look she said, *Now how'd that get there?*

But today Amma was on her best behavior. Having my father on her property brought her prestige in the neighborhood. And so she bowed before him, saying, *I am happy so happy yes so happy to greet you. You stay for a year, sir. If you want, you stay with me for a lifetime.*

My father, of course, understood none of this, but since he guessed that a greeting of sorts was happening, he said the one Sinhala word he knew: "Ayubowan."

*Sinhala!* Amma exclaimed, her fingers on her cheeks. *He speaks Sinhala! You just arrive and already you speak Sinhala! Come, you come with me and eat and we talk about old times in Sinhala.*

Cindy told Amma that my father understood nothing and was tired from his long journey. *He needs to rest, Amma.*

*Nonsense!* she protested, grabbing my dad by the elbow and jerking him uphill to her house. *The poor man is starving! He must eat or he will die. I will take care of him, since his children will not.*

*But, Amma,* I said, running up alongside her, *we just ate a few minutes ago.*

*Lies!* she snorted. *All I ever hear from the two of you is lies lies lies. Now this man is going to eat. Period. End of friendly discussion.*

On our way into Amma's house we passed a tall stack of corrugated asbestos sheeting, the kind used to cover roofs. It had been gathered by her husband to sell in his hardware store in downtown Bandarawela. One time I told him that these asbestos sheets caused cancer in First-World countries, which was why they dumped them so cheaply on poor nations like Sri Lanka desperate for money. I presented him with more examples, like DDT and IUDs and barges of radioactive waste that come courtesy of America and Germany.

"*Why not just sell tile roofs, Mudalali,*"—this was his job title, and thus the name everyone called him—"*or tin roofs? Tin is cheap.*"

He stared at me for a long time, long enough for me to wish I had never opened my mouth. Then he pointed his finger at my heart and said in broken English, "You. You American boy. You think you know us but never, never do you know us. You fly here—very expensive to fly, yes?—and then you pretend poor. Pretend, pretend. You play poor for little while and then you fly fly fly fly back home, back under any roof you want." He pressed his finger into the ribs covering my heart. "Never. Never you tell me what to sell to my people."

We passed the asbestos stack and we passed three mangy dogs, all snarling at the foreign smell of my dad's wing tips. Amma threw a sandal at them (I thought: was that *my* old sandal?) and then led us, barefoot, indoors.

Indoors was the brass museum. Brass elephants, brass horses, brass Buddhas, brass spittoons half-filled with betel spit. Brass was the bank, especially to older Sri Lankans suspicious of BankCeylon, the local bank that gave no interest, whose lines circled the block, whose calculations were computed entirely by hand—and the bank whose tellers lived in the largest homes in Bandarawela.

Amma was pleased to see my dad marveling at the brass. *You may touch, sir. It is the most brass in all Bandarawela, by far, by far. Mr. Jim, show your father the glass case. Full of treasures. We are the envy of Bandarawela for our treasures.*

The "treasures" on one shelf were a row of bizarre dolls that show up in nightmares: their eyebrows plucked, their heads bald, their limbs contorted as if having just fallen from a great height— and all suffocating in clear plastic bags. Beneath them on a lower shelf were other gewgaws: a Coke bottle, a jar of glue, a Frisbee, an empty Marlboro carton. America's trash was Sri Lanka's gold. Peace Corps lore had it that one volunteer threw away her birth control locket, only to find it reappear a few days later in a prominent glass case with two family photographs in its wings. I thought for a flash of telling my dad that story, then remembered that all pelvic matters were strictly off limits between us.

Hanging on the wall above the glass case were eleven calendars. (Sri Lankans love calendars, no matter the year.) My dad's attention went to one, a calendar with storybook illustrations on top and, on the bottom, the Peace Corps logo. I told him to look closer beside the logo.

"Well, I'll be," he said. "It's your name. And Cindy's. How'd you swing that one?"

Amma slapped the opposite wall. *Look here. Look at more treasures. Look at our friend Bob.*

I ignored her and her poster of Bob Marley—yes, dreadlock Rastaman himself, here in the home of old Buddhists—and told my dad about the calendar. Cindy and I had hatched the idea two years earlier when we serendipitously discovered a child's picture book, long out of print. On each of its twelve pages were cartoon animals demonstrating some health lesson, like where to build a latrine in relation to the house and the well. Combining the Sri Lankan love for calendars and illustrations with their health needs, we set to work putting it together. Two years later—after negotiating the rights with the British illustrator, after raising money from American businesses, after finessing our way through the labyrinthine Sri Lankan government—a bullock cart pulled up to our doorstep with twenty thousand calendars. The people of Bandarawela organized an elaborate festival for the distribution, overseen by the head monk (payment: twenty calendars) and catered by Amma (payment: another U2 cassette). All day Cindy and I handed out calendars, and all day we received people worshipping us on their knees.

"These calendars will hang for thirty years," Cindy told my dad, "or more. They're crazy about their calendars."

"Jeez, kids. This sure is quite a—"

*Bob!* Amma slapped the wall louder. *Bob Bob Bob! No one has Bob but we have Bob and all Bandarawela looks up to us. Now come*—she trotted over to my father and grabbed his elbow—*let's go eat.*

"But these calendars. Have you seen—"

*Time to eat, time to eat. Your children starve you, I feed you. Now come. Come eat.*

She continued to accuse me of slowly killing my father until we all sat at the table. It was more platform than table, and Amma insisted that I translate to my dad that thirty could sit here comfortably. *The largest table in Bandarawela,* she boasted. *This is a fact. Every table in town, I know. Every woman in town, I know. And this table*—she pounded it hard—*is the envy of them all. Fact.*

The twelve-year-old Tamil servant, Shamila, entered the room carrying finger bowls of water. Amma tested the temperature of the water and then, her face contorted, bolted to her feet and slapped Shamila hard across the face.

*Cold water!* Amma screamed. *I tell you every time to bring in hot water in those bowls. But no, cold. Always cold. You Tamils, you must like to wash your hands in cold water, keep your hands dirty. Dirty people, all of you. Now, go! Go and make it hot.*

Shamila scurried away, terrified. Soon she would escape like all of Amma's other servants, all Tamil children that Amma had lured away from the neighboring tea estates with promises of comfort and wealth. But for now that promise was getting crushed beneath the weight of a servant's schedule—all day, 5 A.M. to 9 P.M., no breaks, no holidays, no food fit for humans. Shamila ate her scraps alone in the corner of the bleak and smoky kitchen, her frail body blending in with the soot on the walls and the dung on the floor. She was never permitted to sit on a chair. She was never permitted to look into anyone's eyes. Her only peace came during sleep, and that was on a woven mat on the floor, wrapped head to toe in a sheet to defend against rats.

Shamila returned to our table carrying a tray of fresh finger bowls. She stepped back a few feet, trembling, her eyes cast down, while Amma dipped her pinkie into a bowl.

*It's scalding!* Amma shrieked. *You idiot! You little Tamil idiot! I should throw this water into your face and see how it makes you feel. Now go. GO! Out of my sight! Dirt like you does not belong with us.* Amma sighed and smiled her single tooth at my dad. *These Tamils, well, if it weren't for us, for good Sinhalese people like us, they would have no jobs. Cindy, tell the father what I am saying. He must know the truth. These Tamils, they would eat dirt all day, all night*

*without my help. We help them but you see how bad they work. Tell him the truth.*
My dad already knew much of the truth about Tamils from his golden week on the tea plantation. As for Shamila, Cindy told him the truth of her wretched life. "She rarely sees her family, John, and she works fifteen hours each day for hardly any money."

Amma leaned in toward me. *What is she saying, Mr. Jim? Is she telling lies to your good father? You talk, Mr. Jim. You tell the truth.* When I told Amma that Cindy was describing her famous hospitality, she rocked and smiled. *Oh, yes. It is true. It is my nature.*

"Shamila owns one dress," Cindy told my dad, "and that's it, that same dress every day and night. And she carries water half her weight on her head for a half mile, and if she ever spills a drop, Amma goes berserk."

Amma nodded. *Yes, it is true. My hospitality, it is my nature.*

"This poor little girl, she's just a kid, and she gets beat up and starved. The dogs around here are treated better."

*Hospitality and goodness, they come easy to me. I give and I give like the Buddha. People tell me I am like the Buddha. "Amma the Buddha," they say.*

Soon Shamila returned, carrying many dishes of curries on a platter. One curry had spilled slightly over the edge of its bowl, for which Amma clipped Shamila twice across the head.

Amma ladled a mountain of rice onto my dad's plate, encircling it with six large helpings of curried vegetables and fish. When Cindy told Amma that maybe she was overdoing it a bit, Amma ladled on more. *Eat! You must eat until your belly hurts. Eat until the paddy fields are barren. Eat until you sleep and then wake up and I give you more. Eat eat eat.*

My father liked this part of Amma. She fell into a category of women that had recurred throughout his life: buxom, serious about food, a believer that hospitality equals excess, a believer that men are to be fed and that's no funny business. She heaped on more rice.

*Eat eat eat,* she said. *Never stop. Your children don't care for you so I care for you. Why be so shy with food? Eat and eat and eat.*

After a little while my father pushed away his plate with his thumb. "I'm finished, Amma. One more kernel of rice and I'll burst."

She pushed the plate back at him. *You lie. You lie like your children and you talk too much. Fact. Now shut up and eat.*

Eventually she got the point that he really was full. She then called for Shamila, who ran in with eyes wide in terror, wringing her hands on the bottom of her tattered apron.

*Shamila, listen and try to do this right for once. Quarter the papaya and take out every seed but be careful not to get your dirty hands near what we'll eat. And bring it in on the special brass plate that is the envy of every woman in Bandarawela. Now surprise me and get this right.*

The papaya soon arrived in regal fashion, though Amma swatted Shamila because the quarters were cut unevenly. Amma pushed the plate beneath my father's nose. *Eat, sir,* she said. *Eat the papaya and you will have happy bowels. This I know for a fact.*

After eating two large pieces, my dad had me translate to Amma that he'd reached his limit.

Amma scowled. *Then he is a liar just like you, Mr. Jim. He must eat more for the bowels. The more he eats, the more he lets out—this, we old people must know about. Tell him, Mr. Jim. Tell him that I care for his bowels.*

I was relieved of this pleasant duty by the arrival of Mudalali. He entered like a sultan, slowly rubbing his hands across his big belly, a symbol in Sri Lanka of wealth and stature. Upon seeing me he did the same mysterious gesture he always did: He slowly raised his fist to eye level to show me his gold ring, a garish thing the size of a belt buckle. Then he chuckled this deep and ominous chuckle that jiggled his belly. I chuckled, too, like a chum, even though I had no idea what this lunatic was up to.

By instinct my father rose and extended his hand to Mudalali. "Hi there. John Toner. Cleveland, Ohio. That's near Chicago. My son Jimmy here—"

Mudalali did not lift his hand. He turned to his wife and asked, *Has the white man seen the toilets?* She shook her head no. "Then come," he said to my dad. "Come and see my toilets."

My dad turned to me with his hand still dangling in midair. "Did he say something about toilets, Jimmy?"

"Come now," Mudalali said. "Leave the table and come see my toilets." I started to rise with my father until Mudalali put a hand on my shoulder. "Only him. Only the father will see the toilets."

My dad wiped his hands on a napkin. "Well, this is some honor, huh, kids? To travel twelve thousand miles to see a toilet or two." He looked down at me in mock sadness. "Now don't you be jealous, Jimmy. Your day will come to see the toilets, too. All in good time."

Mudalali snapped his fingers at me. *What is your father's job?*

*He's a judge.*

Mudalali liked this answer. *What is his salary?*

I dodged this routine Sri Lankan question by saying that my dad was retired.

*How many toilets in his house?*

"Hey, Dad, how many johns in the condo? Two? Three?"

"Two. Does that disqualify me from the tour?"

"Only two?" Mudalali sneered. He turned toward the corner brass spittoon and—ping!—let fly a jet of red betel juice. "Then I invite you to see my collection."

They were gone long enough for me to worry. I imagined Mudalali, an oily businessman, convincing my dad to send him a crate of alto saxes, maybe a stack of asbestos, perhaps a few drums of DDT. Meanwhile, Shamila returned to wipe up our messes and to endure more Amma abuse—about her dirty hands, about her dirty Tamil family.

A little later the two fathers' voices approached us from down the hall, their banter quick and lively. Maybe I was seeing things, but it looked to me like they were holding hands.

"Jim, Cindy," my dad gushed, "this is something, really something! This guy has . . . what is it, Mudie: twelve? ten?"

"Twelve," he said, his fingers now stroking my father's forearm.

"Twelve toilets! Some are commodes, some squat. You've got your cement, you've got your marble. And, kids, get this: He's got these drawings of gods all over the place. Buddha's the only one I know but, jeesh, this stuff is art, kids. Real art! A little Sistine Chapel right here in every toilet. And some of those animals—holy God!—they look like they'll jump right out at you when you're in that helpless position."

I asked my dad if he was putting me on.

"Putting you on? Kids, these toilets are really something! And as far as I can gather, Mudie here uses them in rotation." The sultan nodded. "He slides a spittoon from door to door to help remember. Now I call that something."

"Tell me you're joking, Dad."

"Just you watch, Jimmy. There's gonna be some big-time renovation in the condo when I get home."

Soon we found some excuse to leave this madness. After passing the brass elephants and Bob Marley and the bald, twisted dolls, we put our shoes back on and headed toward our house. Amma ran behind us, shouting to my father to *eat eat eat* and to stop lying. From back at his front door Mudalali shouted to his wife to shut up, and then, rubbing his big old pregnant belly, reminded my dad to use his toilets. "Any time, night or day. Pick one of my twelve toilets, and enjoy."

We walked downhill through high grass and a grove of banana trees to get to our house. At the doorway my dad removed his wing tips without my instructions, then placed them in a corner as if knowing that they belonged to a different world. Here my dad stood on the threshold of my home, and I wondered if he could find the sacred in a place of so much mud and so much nothing. He looked in. "Jeez, kids," he said, "sure looks . . . cozy."

He stepped his bare feet inside. Here was the meeting of white suburban feet with the mud and the cow dung of a jungle home. He wiggled his toes. He wiggled them some more, and then said, "Feels a wee bit gooey." Inside he ran his hands across the mud walls and, seeing a gecko, rose up on his toes to get a closer look. With his eyes an inch from its transparent tail, my dad said, "Hmm, now isn't that something."

He then followed me into the kitchen, stopping briefly in front of our small Buddha shrine. As he bent down for a closer look I wondered if the words "Jimmy" and "pagan idolater" were combining in his head. But when I saw his fingers at work in his pocket feeling his chipped Buddha, I knew all I needed to know. He said, "Hmm," and then looked down near his feet. "My oh my, will you look at that."

He lowered his stiff, unsteady body onto his knees and then waved me down. "Come here, Jimmy. Come here and take a look." I did, and together we watched a hundred red ants swarming on an overturned cockroach. The ants were carrying it like a funeral procession that moved from room to room, my father and I following behind with our noses to the ground like a pair of hounds. We entered the kitchen where Cindy, who had been grinding chili peppers, put down her heavy rolling stone and joined us on her knees. It was a sight: three big white folks towed by a cockroach's funeral cortege. After leading us outside, where the ants slid their dinner into the earth, my dad raised up and shook his head. "Well well well, that's some kind of show, Jimmy. Such industry, such community. Like the Amish, those fellows."

We stood up. My dad's pants were stained at the knees by cow manure and red dust. He didn't seem to notice, nor did he notice that his pants were all stuck and puckered to his knees. But I did, and when I did I knew that Vijay's words were right: "You'll know when to pass on this gift, Jim, and to whom."

Yes, I knew the gift I would soon give to my dad, but no gifts until this old man from Cleveland had learned some domestic arts. Cracking open and grinding a coconut, cleaning rice, washing clothes by hand—these were activities as alien to him as stacking a dishwasher would be to a Sri Lankan. I placed a coconut in my dad's palm and a dull, heavy knife in the other.

"Now, Dad," I said, "don't go lopping off a thumb. Get it out of the way, that's it, and aim for one of these three ridges. That's it, that's it. Just remember, your whole life in the jungles of Cleveland has prepared you for this one moment. Just pretend the coconut's a skull and whack away."

He arched his eyebrows at me. "A skull? Jimmy, do you have some experience with skulls you'd like to share with me? I am a judge, remember."

I told him to strike away, though I had no confidence at all in him. Every tool in his hands never looked quite right. When I recalled his carpentry history—bloody thumbnails, rusty tools, a bookcase he had once built that collapsed beneath the weight of a few paperbacks—I had good reason to panic. I imagined his severed thumb being carried across the kitchen floor by a thousand ants. I imagined him losing the grip on the knife, sending it into flight over our roof and crashing into Amma's house, burying itself into Mudalali's skull while he squatted over Toilet 6.

"Be careful, Dad," I said. "And don't expect to get the coconut open right away because it takes lots and lots of—"

But suddenly he screamed a Tarzan scream and in one swift confident stroke—thwot!—he split the coconut into two clean halves. He held up both for us to see.

"And that's how it's done," he said, yawning.

"My God, Dad, do you have any idea—"

"Any idea what? Any idea that I'm gifted? Any idea that I just performed a one chopper? That's what we in the business call it, a 'one chopper.' "

I told him to pour a few drops of the coconut water into the earth. "To appease the coconut gods," I said, "wherever they may lurk." He did, and then we passed one of the halves around our circle, each of us taking a sip as if partaking in some blood ritual.

I then led him to the contraption for grinding out the coconut meat. It was the *hiromoni*, a thick block of wood with an arched metal arm nailed into the side. The arm had cobra connotations, both in the way it reared up into a widened head and in the danger of its sharp, serrated teeth. It took a little getting used to, though my father, whose ease with coconuts had already been demonstrated, quickly got the feel for the rhythm and the rotation. While whistling "Stardust" he grated one half and then began the other. I was ready to compliment him until I noticed that he was secretly eating half of the shavings that fell into the bowl, then fluffed up the remains. This was a revelation to me: My dad is a food snitcher. Since I too was a chronic food snitcher, I wondered if it was genetic coding, not weakness of will, that had *forced* me all these years to tunnel into my mom's off-limits potato salad. I would tunnel and eat, tunnel and eat, then manicure the surface, just like my dad, in order to hide what I had just ravaged underneath.

"Dad," I said, "no snitching. I see what you're up to."

He looked up at me with fake sad eyes. "Oh, Jimmy, me lad," he said, pulling out his Irish brogue for sympathy, "I just took a wee taste. Just a wee morsel. Just enough to see if it was tasty for . . . for *your* belly. I did it for you, my son. All for you."

He bribed me with a handful of coconut and I forgave him.

We moved outside to perform another task, this time cleaning the rice. The trick here is to toss the rice into the air using a matted platter called a "winnowing fan." While the rice is in midair the dust blows away so that the pebbles, being heavier, fall to the lower edge of the fan—a miniature version of what Yaseratne had done in the rice fields. It requires a deft hand. I soon realized that my father had no such hand, his rice flying onto the roof and scattering to the ground. In the end all his fan held was a handful of pebbles.

"Hey, I'm a coconut man," he said. "Can't expect a coconut man to bother with such girly business."

After another hour of preparation we ate our meal, the three of us in a circle squatting low on stools a few inches off the ground, holding plates of spicy curries in our laps. By now my father could eat with his fingers like a native. Nothing would fall onto his lap. When a kernel or two would fall onto mine, he'd point and say, "That's a crying shame."

On this day he enjoyed the spicy beans and lentils and dried sardines, but at its end he promised to cook for us a far tastier and more exotic meal the next morning. "The food of the gods," he declared, and at sunrise the next day he unveiled a treasure for us with a dramatic flourish: the box of Bisquick.

"Pancakes, kids. Time for golden pancakes—American style! Now everybody out out out of the kitchen. There's a pancake genius with some serious work to do."

It was true: He knew his pancakes. I remembered as a child when my dad, after Sunday Mass, would flip hubcap-sized pancakes into the air for us seven kids. For me it was magic. Though I knew my dad was a clod in the kitchen—broken yolks, soupy oatmeal, bread cut in rough ways—I also knew that pancakes were a different matter altogether. With a big pancake balanced on the spatula, he'd say, "Ready, Jimmy? Now watch," and flip it up high while spinning on his heels, catching the pancake on the way down in the center of the pan. I'd jump up and down and cheer, for at that moment my dad was slicker to me than my Cleveland baseball hero, Rocky Colavito.

And now, thirty years later near the equator, the Hubcap Pancake had returned. My father carried the plate of oversized, steaming pancakes to us like an offering. We devoured every one with the grace of farm animals. When finished I asked for more, and later even more, until in the end the three of us lolled on our stools, groaning, trying to speak but without enough blood in the brain to create language.

Hours later the idea of standing up began to make sense. We did, and eventually Cindy fetched water from the well for the dishes while I led my father outside to the laundry station. We sat on low benches next to a large flat rock and a cistern filled with rainwater and mosquito larvae. With this infested water we washed our clothes, though "wash" is far too gentle of a word to describe the violence done to laundry in this country. Pulverize, mutilate, crush—this is the Sri Lankan way, twisting the clothes and then bashing them against a rock over and over until the dirt pleads mercy and drips away.

My dad and I bashed away together, the water sloshing up high onto our calves and the lather dotting our chins and elbows.

"Lil oughta be happy she's got a machine," my dad said.

It was hard work, messy work, and next to the contortions required when riding a bus, it was my most strenuous exercise while in Sri Lanka. I instructed my dad to wash in the same spirit he had cut the rice: slowly, in the present only, unaware of how much more there was to do. "Just concentrate on that T-shirt. Only that. Feel your elbows working and feel the water on your arms."

"Teeka-teeka like?" he said.

I laughed. "Yeah, exactly, Dad. Teeka-teeka."

For the next half-hour he lathered and pummeled in a slow and silent way—a meditation, though he'd never use that word. Thinking of that, and seeing that his pants were now soaked through, I put down my laundry and went inside. When I returned I held his gift behind my back. I told my dad to stand and to take off his pants.

"Say what?"

"Just do as I say. Cindy's inside."

He slid off his pants and stood in his sagging white underwear, barefoot and arms sudsy. I told him to close his eyes. He did, and from behind my back I brought out a sarong that I folded around my dad's waist. This was no mere sarong, but a batik one made by Vijay and given to me as a gift. I cherished it more than anything, and in its threads I felt my deep affection for Vijay. I also heard in those same threads his very clear order, "You must give it away someday. A gift becomes valuable when it is given again. You *must* give it away, Jim, and you will know when and to whom."

Though I knew this was the right moment for the gift, I still had a flash of fear in the moment before my dad opened his eyes: He will mock me. He will joke about the sarong going well with his earrings and sequined purse. He might act effeminate and swagger.

But he did none of these things. He opened his eyes and looked straight at me, seeing the spirit of the gift and not the thing. After all those years of obligatory presents from his kids—bottles of Old Spice, more bottles of Old Spice—he finally met a simple gift that came from the heart. While still looking at me he ran his fingers across the sarong, and while still looking at me he said, "It feels warm on me, Jimmy. It feels right on me."

"Hey, Dad," I joked, "maybe Malone'll want to borrow it. Wear it out on the town, out to Swingos or Pier W."

"Yeah, Malone," my dad snorted, still stroking his sarong. "You tell me, Jimmy: What does Malone know about a thing like this?"

Cindy stood in the doorway holding our cassette player, smiling at my father in his new sarong. She set the machine down and hit "play" while I returned to the laundry. It was the sound of Benny Goodman, a tape that had just arrived in a packet from Cindy's mother. For the first time in the history of this jungle, the music of big band America was floating up high into the banana trees and up higher to a sun hanging directly overhead. My dad recognized the song immediately.

"'In the Mood'! My oh my, kids, that's 'In the Mood'! Oh your mother and me, we heard it live, summer of 1940 before the war and all of us out there at Geneva-on-the-Lake. Oh let me tell you, we were dancing, kids. *Dancing!*" His eyes grew wide and bright. "Us and the Breiners and Coughlins and Corrigans, Irene and John. All of us dancing to Benny Goodman himself—live! I'm talking *live!* 'In the Mood' and Lil and me dancing and swinging in the air so fast, so smooth. Oh lordy, now that was livin', kids! That was *dancin'!*"

He tightened his sarong around his waist. "Jimmy, can you give us a little more volume, and Cindy,"—he motioned with his finger—"you come over here."

I leaned over from my stool and turned the dial up high, Benny Goodman rising up to the banana leaves and spreading out into the jungle. And my dad took Cindy by the hand and together they danced, shuffling and twirling and laughing in their bare feet and sarongs while I clapped my sudsy hands and sent bubbles high up into the air.

# 10

Amma stole his left wing tip. She did it down by the river in plain view of everybody. We were there as usual at daybreak in our sarongs, standing calf-deep in water alongside a dozen villagers and a few cows. For all of us this was the morning ritual of ablutions, and my father—he from the land of marble tubs and hot-water taps—loved it. He loved it more each morning of his visit. If we weren't yet awake he would enter our bedroom and tug on my toes. "C'mon, Jimmy," he'd insist, "the sun's up and the cows are waiting so *let's go, let's go, let's go!*" And we would go, trailing a few steps behind him. It was hard to believe: This same man who had dreaded putting ice from the Colombo Lake House in his Scotch was now, a month later, willing to rinse out his mouth with river water. Next to a cow.

On the morning of the wing-tip theft my father made an easy target. He stood among a group of men, all in sarongs and standing barefoot in the river, telling them through my translation about his experience at the Sunday market in town. "I couldn't *give* my money away. Everybody offered me something—mangoes, a bag of rice, more mangoes. The lime lady, she loads me up, and some fellow with pineapples, he loads me up."

Suddenly one of the village men standing next to my dad pointed in fake alarm into the high grass. *Panther, sir,* he whispered, squatting low. We followed the direction of his finger: a banana leaf in the grass, moving toward us, everything well-hidden except for an old lady's rump. *The one-toothed panther is back!*

As the banana leaf tiptoed closer, the men around my father took turns reporting what the panther had recently stolen from them: a sarong, a few bricks, a water buffalo for an hour. *But the panther returns everything,* Lalith said. He reached down to grab one of my father's wing tips and, tossing it at the banana leaf, said more loudly, *Except for one time. A poster. A poster picture of . . . I don't know, some musician. Named Tom, I think.*

Amma suddenly stood up from behind the banana leaf. *It's Bob and you lie! All of you lie! I take nothing and I give everything but you people are just jealous.* She slipped her broad left foot into the wing tip and crouched behind the banana leaf. *You are jealous because my table is so big and we have so much brass. This is a fact.*

Lalith asked her to drop the leaf and come out in the open. *Amma, you know what they say: A bikini cannot hide an elephant.*

She walked away from the river and from everybody's laughter, hobbling along in her left wing tip. When she reached the crest of the embankment she stopped and, lowering the banana leaf to her nose, glared down at us. *Just remember,* she said. *My husband has twelve toilets. This is a fact. And remember: The white sir is my friend. He speaks Sinhala to me. He eats my papayas. I help with his bowels.*

After Amma left, the river conversation turned to the rice harvest and to the repair of the temple roof, and after a while, to whether my dad should remain in Bandarawela, forever.

By noon the left wing tip was back on our doorstep, stretched in the middle and flecked with dirt. It arrived just in time for our mile walk to DELIC, the District English Language Improvement Center in which Cindy and I taught. On this final day in Bandarawela, two days before his flight back to Cleveland, my father would see me as a teacher for the first time in his life.

I was worried. It was one thing for him to observe me washing clothes and worshipping Buddha and speaking Sinhala; it was quite another for him to see me at my life's focal point, doing what a thousand life choices had led me to do. I was neither priest nor lawyer, and no matter how proud I was of being a Peace Corps teacher, the sad truth was that this man, this weak old man, still held the power to wither me with one yawn and one glance at his watch.

The walk to school was uphill and hot. What had been our lively parade route was now, at noon beneath the unbearable sun, completely deserted. No people, no animals, no wind. The heat of the sun was now a heavy thing, its weight pressing down on my shoulders and the banana leaves. In the shadow of one tree lay a dog with more scabs than hair, its eyes half opened to make sense of these three tall whites carrying umbrellas, their shoes pulling up strands of melted asphalt with each step. But there was no sense to be made of any of this, so the dog, covering its face with crossed paws, fell asleep.

No buses passed. I kept imagining that I heard one approaching, but when I turned to look all I saw was the hazy smoke of heat. I was irritable, I was tired, yet during it all my seventy-four-year-old father never complained. A lizard darting across the road fascinated him, as did the utter silence of the heat, as did the road itself, a road made of pebbles that hundreds of women had chipped out of boulders. My dad asked questions about it all. And he asked about the peculiar pink and turquoise car approaching us.

It was Mudalali's car. For once I was happy to see the lunatic, assuming he had come to rescue us from the one-hundred-degree heat. We closed our umbrellas as he slowed down near us, slow enough for us to hear his sinister laugh, slow enough for us to see his garish gold ring that he displayed out the window as his car met us and as his car, without us, sped away.

"The fat bastard," Cindy snarled.

We took turns imagining tortures for Mudalali—Shamali in leather, whipping his belly and blowing asbestos fibers down his throat—until another travel option appeared downhill, rounding a curve. It was a private van bulging with passengers, sputtering uphill through a black cloud of exhaust. People were crammed into its belly and were swarming all over its skin. "My God," my dad said, "it looks like a cockroach covered with ants."

At about the time I was thinking, "When he starts coming up with similes like that, he's been in Sri Lanka too long," the van died alongside of us. Without a word of complaint the passengers stepped onto the road, dozen after dozen of them as if part of some magic act. When the van was empty the driver went to work, unhooking a spare gas can from behind the rear seat and inserting a siphon into its spout. Then he crawled backwards out of the van and stood right in front of me, his eyes fixed onto mine while he tipped the tube to his lips.

I wanted to scream. When the gas began dribbling out the sides of his mouth he smiled at me, smiling to make sure I got a good hard look at the poison that was his life: chained to the monotony of the same five-mile route day after day, year after year, heat upon heat. And for that his reward was a few coins and a mouthful of gas. From above the can of gas his eyes burned into mine, and suddenly I became too aware of my ironed shirt and clean fingernails and white skin. "Tell me," those fierce eyes were demanding of me, "tell me what you know of the taste of gas. Tell me, you American humanitarian, what good you are in my country teaching the tongue of an invader when the problem is right here in my mouth, killing me."

He was striking too close to the mark. Like a good little coward I walked away from him and the thought, turning my attention to my own dry throat. Cracked as dried leaves, I thought. Aside from the sweat falling into my eyes and the mirage of Lake Tahoe up ahead, this was a world without water. Smoke rose off the asphalt like stirred ash. Out of the periphery of one eye I could see my father, sagging, sucking the last drops out of Big Green, and out of the other eye I could see the glint of sunlight off wet glass.

Wet glass?

I looked to the side of the road, and there against an avocado tree leaned a bottle of Fanta, beaded with its own melting ice. Now this, for sure, *was* a mirage, a cruel trick of the mind that had me fantasizing about Fanta on the brink of dehydration.

I reached out for it. In the moment before touching it, though, I heard through the silence of the heat a squeaking shutter from the house behind the avocado tree. In the flash before the shutter closed I glimpsed the hand of mute Nishanka retracting like a tongue into the darkness of her room. I looked back down at the Fanta, now knowing that this was no mirage.

"Dad," I said, picking up the bottle, its chill glass stinging my hot palm, "I think this is meant for you."

Our students ran to meet us as we approached the DELIC. Chandrika, a twenty-year-old woman wearing, like all the women, a formal sari and her hair in a bun, offered us juice and poured water into Big Green; Aruna, wearing the male uniform of a white shirt, ironed slacks, and closed leather shoes, took our book bags off our shoulders without asking.

From their smiles and their energy my father gathered his first impression of a Sri Lankan student, some of whom had traveled two hours to get here. They loved us and they loved school, an enthusiasm that always surprised me because I was so accustomed to the groaning of the American schoolboy, his attention most alert when counting the days to the next holiday. Free days, early

174

dismissals, late starts—the events that an American schoolboy celebrated were, to a Sri Lankan, reasons to grieve. For example, I once announced to my class that the DELIC would be closed for three days because of a politician's assassination.

"But, sir," a woman protested, "why three? One day, yes, or one afternoon, but not three. He is dead, sir. Let us get on with the living."

Another student pleaded, "We can meet at the cricket ground, sir. No one will know. We will bring plenty of food and umbrellas. You can teach us outside."

"Sir, we cannot wait three days. That is impossible."

"We beg of you, sir."

By contrast, the attitude of the typical American teenager toward school is best represented by the tale of Brother Free-Day. I once told this story to Kamalendren, my favorite DELIC student, while we sat in his mud hovel on a tea estate with his two sons, one of whom was severely disabled and who passed the day carving elephants out of wood. Brother Free-Day, I said, was this ancient monk who tottered through the halls of my Catholic boys' high school in Cleveland, his fading health the concern of every student. We all knew that the day he died would be a day we had no school; hence the name. He had outlived my first three years in high school, and now as seniors our fear was that he'd die after graduation. This concerned us more than our college applications.

"Hello, Brother Free-Day," we'd greet him in the halls. "It's ten below outside, perfect for a stroll. Perfect for ice fishing. Ever try ice fishing, Brother?"

He'd smile vacantly, clinging to a walker and wheezing heavily. We kept close track of that wheeze.

In late winter, between quarters of a varsity basketball game, the principal announced with great sorrow that Brother Free-Day had passed away that afternoon. Immediately, eight hundred white American teenage males erupted into wild cheers, stomping their feet and chanting, "BROTHER FREE-DAY! BROTHER FREE-DAY! BROTH—..."

I laughed in Kamalendren's house at the recollection of this story, then noticed, for the first time, that he and his children were not amused. They were staring at me, a little bewildered and a little disturbed. The disabled child's whittling knife froze above his elephant.

"I'm sorry, sir," Kamalendren said soberly. "I think I understand your English but maybe I do not. Please repeat the story, sir."

I did, this time actually mimicking Brother Free-Day hobbling across the room, leaning heavily on an imaginary walker. I waited for Kamalendren to finish his Tamil translation to his sons, expecting an uproarious laughter from all three. It never came.

Kamalendren sat forward on his chair. "I'm sorry, sir. You say you want this man to die, and you want to ... to ... avoid, is that the English word? Avoid school?"

"Exactly. Isn't that hysterical?"

He paused. "What is so good outside school that you want a man to die?"

"No, no, no, Kamalendren," I laughed. "You see, he dies—"

"He dies and you are punished."

"Oh, no. Don't you see? He dies and we are *rewarded*. We *don't* go to school. Get it?"

But there was no getting it. All three continued to stare at me, more and more guardedly, as if I were the carrier of an infectious disease that threatened their tribe. I was relieved when Kamalendren's wife brought in a tray of hot *wadee*s and we began to discuss tea prices.

Word soon spread at DELIC that the old white man with the Totes umbrella was my father. Students began to crowd around him in a circle without touching him, remaining a few feet back as if his prestige were a protective moat. It fell to Kamalendren as the eldest student to step forward and address my father in English.

"To sir, most honored sir," he said, bowing at the waist, "I give welcome to our country and to our DELIC. Your Mr. Jim and your Miss Cindy, they are our teachers. They change our lives. It is our dream to someday like them teach children, too, and then we change lives. Because you are their father, it is to you that we give our greatest—"

"Get away! All of you get away now. I say! Go go *go!*"

We swiveled our attention to the shrill voice coming up the hill. It was Aira Ellipola, our principal, trudging her thick, squat body toward us. "I will have *no idlers* at my school. Is that clear! Now all you *lazy idlers*, go go go, out of my sight!"

It was 2:45 in the afternoon and Aira was, as usual, late. The Education Ministry had set our hours from 1:30 to 6:00, yet Aira and the other three teachers seldom arrived before 2:30 and usually left by 5:00. A complete afternoon of English classes, then, would shrink to just two hours, from which another thirty minutes would be sliced off for a tea break and for "adjustment periods" on either side of that tea break. "Adjustment period" was Aira's invention. She was proud of it. "All of the DELICs now have adjustment periods," she often boasted. "Everyone wonders how we lived so long without them."

At the sound of Aira's roar the students quickly scattered, afraid that she might single one of them out for public punishment.

"Kamalendren!" she shouted. "Never socialize! You are here to work and not to play. Is that clear?"

"Yes, Madam."

"All work, no play."

"Yes, Madam."

"Now go. Go to class and stop all this silliness."

Aira Ellipola ("Some call me the 'Iron Lady' but my heart is soft as a gumdrop") was a tyrant. While strolling the school grounds she greeted no one, ignoring all the students who stood rigidly at attention until she passed. She carried an umbrella but never any

177

books. That was Gita's job. Gita was a young teacher, hand-picked by Aira for her meekness and obedience and, above all, for her sharp eye for fresh vegetables. On Tuesdays and Fridays she was excused from teaching so she could buy Aira's vegetables in town.

There were two other DELIC teachers, but neither arrived on this day. One had been gone for three weeks, using some of his forty-five annual sick days to harvest his spring rice. Because he had no replacement, his classes would sit idle, as would the other teacher's, as would Gita's, as would Aira's. Though ordered by the education ministry to teach, Aira refused. "How can I teach with mounds of paperwork to do," she'd complain, fanning herself while Gita, pulled from her own classes, did all the paperwork.

Of the six classes, then, only two got taught. For a while Cindy and I tried to teach both the others and ours simultaneously by straddling classes, or combining them, or leaving some with written work. But Aira ordered the practice stopped. "The students will expect too much of us after you leave," she explained. "You must stop the practice immediately."

We obeyed, but all I could think about were the Kamalendrens out there. His daily commute to DELIC took two hours each way, a journey of long mountain walks and twisting bus rides that brought him, exhausted and poorer, to a school whose teachers were busy buying vegetables in town. But he never complained. Classes or no classes, he would become a teacher in one more year, a position in Sri Lanka just a shade beneath a Buddhist monk in status.

On the day of my father's visit, Aira was in vintage form. She stormed into the office and snapped an order to Gita in English. "Go fetch Wasantha! Get that girl Wasantha in here now!"

"But, Madam," Gita said, "my classes are about to—"

"Your classes can wait! In fact, all classes can wait." She settled in behind her desk, a colossal structure that wrapped around her and spread out before her. Our desks, by contrast, were little satellites of hers. A dictionary, a paper or two, one elbow—that was my desk's holding capacity, all tilting forward because my thighs couldn't fit beneath. "Gita, go tell everyone to gather outside my door and bring Wasantha in here immediately. Bring the pig to slaughter, Gita. Don't just sit there, woman! Go!"

I knew the ugly scene that was coming. To shield my father from it, I led him outside to chat with the students before I returned to our teachers' "meeting" in the office. Aira was growling about something, but I just stared through the warped glass of the office as all the students gathered around my dad, who was sucking on Big Green. I listened to my father's Sri Lankan tales of harvesting rice and opening coconuts, of visiting temples and wearing a sarong. For every question asked of him—"What is your favorite food?" "Is your wife beautiful?" "Can you please stay in my house for a month?"—my father would ask one of his own: "Do you know what pancakes are?" "Were any of your marriages arranged?" "Did you ever see the man in the moon?"

I marveled at this scene, at this improbable but sweet scene of my father interacting on his own with people from another hemisphere. In yet another role reversal, I felt a parent's satisfaction at my child's show of independence. But that pleasant thought ended when Wasantha, her eyes down, her armpits widely ringed with sweat, entered the office and stood before Aira. "You called for me, Madam?" she whispered.

"Did I call for you!" Aira hollered, her red eyes bulging and her body straining forward across the platform desk. "Do you think I made a mistake and called the wrong girl!"

"I'm sorry, Madam. I—"

"Shut up! Shut up and sit down, little girl!"

Wasantha, a mother of two, sat like a child herself on a small wobbly stool and stared down at her hands. She squeezed and twisted those hands during the five agonizing minutes that Aira remained silent.

179

"My sources tell me," Aira finally said, even-toned, "that you were seen walking in town with another boy."

Wasantha looked up in disbelief. "But, Madam, I never—"

"Shut up! Shut up this instant! If you say 'but' then you call me a liar and I will not stand for that, not from a little rodent like you. You are calling me a liar, is that right?"

"No, Madam. I would never—"

"Shut up!"

"But, Madam, please listen to my—"

"SHUT UP!"

Cindy snapped her pencil. This snap was the loudest protest we could voice. If we were to question Aira's authority and judgment, if we were to protect any of the Wasanthas accused every day in this room, then Aira would banish us from town as she had done to the last three Peace Corps volunteers. We kept quiet, and in so doing we were able to accomplish one simple goal: We stayed. During our two years in Sri Lanka we cured no malaria, built no bridges, doubled no crop production. In the end our biggest achievement may simply have been that we stayed. We swallowed this American impulse to protest so that each year we could teach English and teacher preparation to one hundred eager Sri Lankans—and to teach with a buoyancy that their lives lacked.

Aira's interrogation of Wasantha grew in volume and humiliation. For relief I looked out the warped window. There was my father, towering over everyone else like a silo, mesmerizing the crowd with a story told in fine, Irish raconteur form. During a moment's break in Aira's tirade, I thought I heard him utter the word "diarrhea." When I heard it again, I began to worry.

Aira pointed her finger at Wasantha like a spear. "So it is the truth, my child. You were with a boy in the middle of Bandarawela, and I don't care if he is your cousin. A boy is a boy. The whole town saw it, so now the whole town laughs at me and laughs at my

DELIC. Believe me, child: For eight years my reputation has been pure. No little rodent like you will change that."

While Aira stopped to reload her guns, I again heard "diarrhea" outside. Then "Saint Henry's," then "miracle," then "good as dead," and with those clues I winced at the story my dad was telling my students: the myth of Withering Infant Jimmy, a tale of pure Toner propaganda. A hundred students huddled closer to my dad to hear every word.

Aira cleared her throat. "Wasantha, I am at times soft as a gumdrop, but with you I must be iron. It is my duty, my difficult duty . . ."—Aira paused long enough to see Wasantha digging her nails into her palm—"to expel you immediately from DELIC. Please go, child. Go and take your shame with you."

Wasantha exploded into tears. Her lifetime dream of becoming a teacher had vaporized in a flash. "But, Madam," she sobbed, dropping to her knees, "I beg of you to please have mercy—"

"It is not enough. You come with your parents. They are also to blame. If you come all together and all beg to me on your knees, then . . . perhaps. Perhaps I will turn to gumdrop."

"But, Madam, you know that my parents, they live twelve hours away. They cannot afford to . . ."

Aira casually turned the page of her newspaper. "They come or you go. Quite simple. You should have thought of the trouble you now cause your parents before you did such a foolish thing. You are a selfish child. A very very selfish child. You shame everyone. You are"—Aira laughed—"a shame machine."

I wanted to scream. I wanted to heave my tiny satellite desk across the room and crush Aira. Instead I just smiled and looked to the light and the oxygen outside the warped window, and there, cradling Big Green like an infant, was my father, saying, "Poor little fellow. He was just . . . oh, just a few days old, little Jimmy, and there he was at death's door, nothing but skin and bones. Diarrhea.

That's what the little fellow had." My students' expressions shaded with concern. "Everything little Jimmy ate came splat right out of him."

I was trapped: the tyrant Aira inside, the impressionable students outside picturing me as a baby lying in a puddle of my own mud. Wasantha, meanwhile, was out of control at Aira's feet, blubbering apologies in between great heaving sobs. She planted thick kisses on Aira's shoes.

Aira ignored her. "Gita," she said calmly, turning the newspaper, "did you remember to get me my eggplant? You know I wanted five hundred grams of eggplant this week for my brinjol curry. Some say I make the finest brinjol curry in Bandarawela, but," Aira smiled, "I am only as good as my eggplant." She folded her newspaper in half and stared down at Wasantha, still keening at her feet. "And as for you, all I can say is that I hope you're not getting my shoes wet! Now, Gita, please return to town for my eggplant. I must go talk to all the students about Wasantha's shame."

Aira stood and sidestepped the heap on the floor. Outside I heard my father say, "Good as dead, that's the truth. Hard to believe that such a big boy like my Jimmy was nothing more than a peanut shell. But he was, and he was dying quick, so we took him over to Father Flaherty at St. Henry's near 175th and Harvard, in Cleveland, that's near Chicago. So Lil and I, that's my wife—sweet gal, my Lil—there we stood with wrinkled Jimmy in our palm begging Father Flaherty—"

The office door flew open. All students snapped to military attention, and my dad froze in midsentence.

"A girl has shamed me," Aira proclaimed from the doorway, slowly surveying the crowd. From our vantage point standing behind her, Cindy and I could see Aira's hands clasped around her back; we could see the tightening of every student's face; we could see my father retreat into the crowd. Amid all of this I had a moment to

182

wonder why my parents took me to Father Flaherty instead of to the hospital. "My sources saw this girl walking in town with a boy, and for this, shame now visits me. Everywhere I go—to the temple, to my relatives, to the market to buy my famous eggplant—that is what I shall feel: shame. All because of one selfish child who ignored her culture and ignored her elders. Horrible shame. People will spit on me when I walk through town. And this, my students, this is what I get for sacrificing my life . . . for you. Shame. Enough shame to bury me."

She revolved her body (like the turret of a tank, I thought) and brushed aside Cindy and me as if we were no more than a curtain of beads. She returned to the bunker of her desk and unfolded the newspaper. "Cindy and Jim," she said from behind the paper, "please come sit."

We did, though I lingered at the door just long enough to see the students flock back to my dad, all anxious to hear the end of Withering Infant Jimmy. "As I was saying," he continued, "Lil and I handed to Father Flaherty our little Jimmy no heavier than a paper bag, and we begged him for help. He held our Jimmy all shriveled like a rotten peach in the palm of his hand and said in his Irish way, 'Ahhh, Jimmy me boy, you be cryin' to wake up the divil, that you are. Whooshit, lad, and give the divil his shuteye. Whooshit now. I've got me hands full as 'tis without the divil comin' to visit me, all cantankerous-like from no sleep."

Aira, meanwhile, was waiting for the payoff to her speech. Eventually it arrived in the form of Malik, tiptoeing into the office toward Aira, who was barricaded behind her newspaper and desk. He knelt in front of her and said in English to the floor, "Madam, gracious and ever-kind Madam, your shame is my shame. Please punish me. Punish me for the sins of everyone." He kissed her feet, stood, and by the quickness with which he fled the room, I knew that all he really cared about was the end of Withering Infant

Jimmy. Through the warped glass I watched Malik wedge into the crowd to get closer to my father.

"Father Flaherty," said my dad, raising Big Green to the heavens, "he takes our Jimmy all withered down to nothing, you see, and holds him up in the church to the statue of Christ. 'Sweet Jasus,' he says, 'can I be trooblin' you to let this little one live? His food, it be squartin' out his bottom, you see. Squartin' and squartin'. Jasus, can you ploog up his wee little stinky bottom and end the squartin'? Let the lad live to eat and to play and, God permitting, to take a nip of the Guinness ever so often.'"

Another student followed Malik into the office, kneeling and begging, then another, and another, all groveling below the figure of Aira reading her paper. "Madam," a woman pleaded, "please allow me to accept all your shame. I want your suffering. I want the spit of the townspeople."

Aira turned the page. "I must have my eggplant, Gita. Please go now and don't forget: five hundred grams. Look to see there are no worms. I must have no worms in my famous brinjol curry."

Outside, the students inclined toward my father to hear the much-anticipated ending. "So, after Father Flaherty finished praying," my dad said, "he handed my Jimmy over to me with a wink. 'Johnny,' he says, ''tis the end of the squartin' and the start of the eatin'. Just remember: Be careful what you be praying for, lad, because you just might end up gettin' it.' And sure enough, my Jimmy, he lived that day and lived from then on, and by God he's been eating me out of house and home ever since."

At the grand news of my survival the students cheered, a sound which startled Aira out of her chair. "What is the commotion, Gita? What is the celebration on this sad dark day of shame?" She stepped on the hands of a prostrate student on her way toward the door. "Some heads will roll for this, Gita! I will find the ringleader and I assure you, Jim and Cindy and Gita, I assure you that he will regret he ever knew the Iron Lady. DELIC is not a circus! The ringleader, I will put him on display!"

The ringleader was sipping from Big Green, grinning at his story, unaware that Aira was standing in the doorway with hands on hips. "Who is it?" she shouted into the crowd of students. They all froze, as if this were some twisted version of red light, green light we were all playing. "Tell me: Who is the rat who thinks he is so funny? The comedian. Who is the comedian on this black day at DELIC? Come to the front and make me laugh, Mr. Clown." Nobody moved. "We will stand here in the hot sun until Mr. Clown comes out of hiding. You remember when I made you stand for five hours? This time it will be *five days!*"

At first my dad looked over both shoulders for Mr. Clown. Then, by the slow way he retreated into the crowd, I knew it was dawning on him who the fugitive Mr. Clown was.

"I will not wait!" Aira shrieked. "For every minute it takes Mr. Clown to appear, I choose a student, any student, and out he goes. Expelled! Out of school forever, never to be a teacher." She began to count down from sixty. "I will not be shamed by Mr. Clown. Twenty, nineteen, eighteen . . ."

When she reached three my dad stepped forward, his hand raised. "I must say something, ma'am."

"No, no, no, sir," Aira said, looking embarrassed. "It is not for you to identify Mr. Clown."

"You don't understand. You see—"

Suddenly Kamalendren pushed himself forward from the rear. "It is me, Madam. It is me the comedian." He dropped to his knees at her feet. "I accept your punishment, Madam. You must punish Mr. Clown."

I ached for this man, for this gentle father and husband who endured an epic journey every day to bring himself to this humiliation, who would risk his dream of becoming a teacher just to save

185

face for my father. For some reason Aira looked not at Kamalendren but at my father, and from his expression she quickly realized the entire story.

She lifted Kamalendren by the arm. "Go to class, Kamalendren. All of you, do you hear me? Go to class and stop this idling. You cannot get anywhere in this world without English, so go! Stop staring at me and go to class!"

The classroom was so crowded that most students sat two per chair. When Cindy, my dad, and I entered the room, everybody stood and then waited for my father's permission to sit. It took a while because his attention had turned to the wildlife in the room: the cow with its head looped over the wall, the dog running between students' legs, the crows flying in from the open sides of the room and then resting on the roof beams. A goat strained its neck over the wall to reach some chalk, and when my dad asked it if it knew Malone, it raised its head as if to give it some thought.

Some students laughed at this silliness until others hushed them, apparently having concluded that my dad was somewhat of a lunatic. Throughout the next hour of his visit I kept overhearing this debate—*Oh, he's just joking* versus *oh, no, the poor man's not all there*—and it started with our first class activity. We arranged the students in a circle and instructed them to blindly tear a sheet of paper behind their backs into the shape of an elephant. Everyone giggled at the idea, and then giggled more when I told them that the prize for the best elephant would be the services of my father for six months.

"I'll harvest your rice," he said. "I'll just strap myself to the water buffaloes and get it all done in no time."

I overheard a nearby student whisper, *You see what I mean? The poor old man is quite insane.*

I told the class the two rules to the game: to speak English only, and to not look behind their backs. They all nodded very seriously and then, five seconds later, were all cheating and sneaking glances—but at least doing it all in English. The worst cheater was Reverend Yassassi, the one Buddhist monk in our class, who was twisting around in his saffron robe and asking students for help.

"Reverend," I said, wagging my finger, "no cheating."

"Just a little peek, Mr. Jim. My elephant, he has sad legs."

"But, Reverend, you know that cheating is a sin."

"Sin? Ah, yes: sin. But don't you know," he winked, "that we Buddhists have a very happy notion of sin. Now please, Mr. Jim, please come help me sin and help me get my trunk right."

And I did, partly because all the nearby students insisted on it— "Help the Reverend, Mr. Jim, help him so he wins your father, and he makes your father a Buddhist monk"—and partly because he was one of my closest friends. He had taught Cindy and me about Buddhism, and especially, in our many visits to his monastery, about his life as a monk. He once told us that his only sadness as a monk came at age five. "My mother brought me to the monastery. I let go of her hand and ran fast, very fast all around the temple, until my teacher, he stops me. Never, he says, never again can I run. Monks don't run, ever. And I cry and cry because I am a boy and I love to run. Yes, I was very sad that day, and that was the last day I ever run. Ever."

My dad, meanwhile, was tearing his elephant with the silence and concentration of a safecracker. When I asked him how he was doing, he hushed me up quick. "Please, can't you see there's an artist at work." He stared intently into a pocket of space a few feet out from his navel. "I *see* the elephant, son. In fact, I *am* the elephant."

In the end we told everyone to hold their elephants on their heads. Most resembled locomotives or amoebas. My father's was more a seven-legged toaster, which the class politely admired. "It's the *soul* of an elephant," he explained, and those who thought my dad already insane just nodded in a knowing way.

My dad's blob contrasted with the winner, Reverend Yassassi, whose elephant was detailed with eyelids and floppy ears and tusks, and which bore the clear marks of the class artist, Manjula. I asked the Reverend if he'd like to tell the class anything.

"Yes, Mr. Jim. Your father, he is my prize, and I will make him a Buddhist monk in six months. In six months he returns to America in yellow robe and bald head."

"What do you think of that, Dad? You a monk roaming the streets of Cleveland?"

"Well, sure, why not? I think it's time I gave those priests over at Saint Luke's a run for their money. And besides, I look good in yellow and my hair could sure use a trim."

We ended the game with everyone trumpeting one robust elephant call. It wasn't much of a surprise a minute later when Gita arrived at the doorway carrying a note from Aira. I imagined Aira's fury at our elephant games, her fingertips drumming across her vast desk. I imagined her looking down to her shoes and, seeing no one groveling or sobbing, deciding to control the sky. "Storm is coming," her note read. I leaned out over the railing and saw a cloudless sky. "Send students home in ten minutes." I assured Gita that we would be leaving soon, but she wasn't listening to me. Her attention was on the paper elephants, and then on both my father and Reverend Yassassi imitating elephants. She smiled and lingered until I told her gently that Aira was probably waiting for her to return.

As usual, we stretched the ten minutes out to an hour—still two hours short of the full school day. I'm not sure in two years I ever experienced a full school day, not with the JVP declaring a curfew or with the sudden bursts of the monsoon or with the army raiding the school to "disappear" a handful of male students. Usually, though, it was just Aira: Aira tired, Aira in need of vegetables, Aira in a rage. With the little clout Cindy and I had as white Americans, the best we could do was to delay the order.

On this day we filled the delay with more games. There was a mix of Jeopardy ("Mr. Jim, I'll take 'Prepositions' for fifty.") and bingo ("past tense of 'drink'" to find on a verb card) and grammar baseball ("That's correct, Kamalendren. Now you get to throw the tennis ball at the goat.") My father participated in each game, and though I wondered what any of this could mean to him—his son, the goofy teacher—I knew from his ease and involvement that he understood my madness. Language was in full use, loud and from every mouth, even though it appeared secondary to winning a toss at a goat. The pleasure of play was my strategy as a teacher, a pleasure my father now knew well from running with Rufi and from finger games on a train with a slobbering boy.

I stopped to watch him. He shared a seat with Kamalendren, the two of them intently searching their bingo card for "drunk," and the two of them sagging when Reverend Yassassi bolted up, shouting, "BINGO!" with a card he'd doctored into winning. When I split the class into groups to debate the merits of arranged marriages, my dad joined in on the debate, too. "Yes, that may be true," he said, "but you still have to put faith in love, in falling in love." His group got off track when he explained the expression "falling in love," and deeper off track when he recounted the first time he laid eyes on my mother. "My heart was beating so loud I thought it'd leap out of my chest, and when I first heard her laugh, I knew, I just *knew* I wanted to hear that laugh the rest of my life."

Gita entered the room without my noticing and, trembling, handed me a new, emphatic note from Aira. I looked over at my father—"That sweet laugh had nothing to do with the *business* of marriage . . ."—and then headed for the office.

"Aira, please. A few more minutes and we'll be about done."

"About done! An hour ago I politely, *very* politely, told you that a storm was—"

"I know, I know. And the storm will be here any day but you see, it's my dad. He just wants to say a few things to the class and then we'll be gone."

I had her. In this hierarchical society, Aira may have towered above the students, but my dad—my white old male American dad—was as far above Aira as the sun is above a worm. For today, my dad called the shots. When I told Aira, "Oh, and my father made a special request for Gita to stay in the class," she crossed her arms and turned away.

I met Gita in the hallway and grabbed her by the elbow. "Aira's orders," I said, and together we returned to the classroom where we joined the circle in song. This time it was their favorite, Harry Belafonte's "Day O," a nice relief from their usual insistence on "Where Have all the Flowers Gone" and (oh, the horror, the horror) "Kumbaya." The song didn't matter to them. As long as the tune was American, no monsoon could pry away a singing Sri Lankan.

On one side of the circle was my father, Day O—ing like Belafonte himself, and on the opposite side was Gita. In two years I had never seen her like this. She had shed the usual terror in her face and, clapping and swaying and belting out "Daylight come and I wanna go home," she had become a little girl again. Gone for this brief moment were the hard edges of her jaw, the bowing of her shoulders. She reminded me of what the soldiers at the checkpoint could have been if they had hopped over the Lemon Twist cord, all of them suddenly children at play, all of them briefly stepping off the stage of their sad dark drama.

When the song ended, Gita insisted we repeat it. "Again and again. 'Day O' will teach us good English, but only with practice. Begin." We did, over and over, until Gita stepped forward and asked my father for a new American song. "These students need to learn more English, sir. Please sing for us and we will learn."

"Sure," he said, clearing his throat. "No harm in that. Let's see . . . well, one of my favorites doesn't really have a name but we'll just call it 'The Banana Song.'" He nodded to me as if I were a lounge pianist in a Holiday Inn. "Jimmy, help me get 'em rolling," and together we sang: "Yes, we have no bananas. We have no bananas today. We have cherries, apples, pears. But—ho, ho, ho—we have no bananas today."

At first I wanted to apologize to the cow and the goat and to every student for this lowbrow sample of Western music. But they were applauding—loud applause, rock-concert applause. Even the cow tilted its head in some vague show of interest. After we all belted out the tune three or four times, my dad raised his hand. "Well, well, well," he said, "if it's a classic American song you're after, well, look no further than 'The Hokey-Pokey.'"

Cindy half-moaned, half-laughed. "Just watch. They'll forget everything we ever taught them and take 'The Hokey-Pokey' out to every village in the jungle."

I marveled at the scene: Kamalendren putting his left foot in, Gita putting her left foot out; the Reverend putting his left elbow in, Wasantha putting her left elbow out—and then all hundred of them twirling and singing, "You sing the Hokey-Pokey and you turn it all around, that's what it's all about—clap, clap!" On one rotation I thought I saw, in a flash so swift I doubted my own eyes, the slightest corner of Aira's face peering in from the corridor, but on second look she was gone.

The students were giddy. Part of their pleasure came from getting the inside scoop on the great American culture, but I think more of the joy came from a rarer pleasure: seeing an old respected white man being silly right in front of them. Following his lead they shook their noses and earlobes, their butts and ankles, and each time their lips wrapped around this new "Hokey-Pokey" sound, they broke into hysterics.

I stopped to admire it all, the hundred dark faces of my students in the fading afternoon light, all obeying an old white man from another world, all smiling in this safe pocket of a circle while not too far away their country was shredding itself apart. Outside this circle were burning tires and green Mitsubishi jeeps speeding toward this classroom. But here inside for a short while was something sacred and immortal and pure, and leading it all was—how preposterous!—Judge John Toner of Cleveland, Ohio. This circle of song and dance brought to mind all our other circles during the month: the circle of Rufi's family beneath a full moon, the circle of Tamils near Vijay's house singing "wanacome," the circle of our meal on low benches around a hearth.

I turned to my dad. Between his "Hokey-Pokey" gestures I flattened his white wild hair and buttoned an undone button in the middle of his shirt. We linked arms, and together arm-in-arm we twirled and we sang, "That's what it's all about—clap, clap!"

A louder "clap-clap" from outside the circle drew my attention. There stood Aira, smiling. As soon as she realized I was watching, she quickly erased her smile and wiped her hands on her sari. But it was too late. In that half-second before she could replace her mask, I had seen Aira as a little schoolgirl just wanting to be included in our circle of play. Oh, how I wanted to swoop her up in my arms and trumpet our silliest elephant calls and then set her down in the center of our circle. Instead I stiffened, bracing myself for her inevitable rage.

"Mr. Jim," she said. Her voice was soft, and the students, some frozen in midtwirl, looked bewildered at a tone they'd never heard emanate from that mouth. "This 'Hokey' song. It is a good English lesson and so some day you must teach me. Of course it is not as good as 'Day O' but what song is? Now, it is getting dark. Let your father say some words and then we absolutely must dismiss. Now, where is Wasantha?"

Wasantha took a step back and dropped her eyes. "Yes, madam?"

"You sit with me, here, and let us listen to our honored guest." She clapped twice. "Now sit down everyone and listen well. Wasantha, you must listen to the elders if you are to be a teacher. Now come sit by me."

As we all found seats to share, my father stood alone in front of the class, his hands plunged deep into his pockets. Rosary beads and a chipped Buddha—that's what he was fingering in those pockets. This, I thought, is no Saint Luke's sports banquet. This is no basement of a grade school with my dad speaking on stage and I am not ten years old eating bad sausage and bad scrambled eggs that came from a carton. No, this is a moment with weight—coming as it does near the end of his life, coming as it does near the end of his knowing about my life.

"You know," he began, scanning the hundred black faces fixed onto his face, "I really didn't come here to make a speech. 'Hokey-Pokey'—that's about the wisest thing I can come up with today. But still, I just want to say how honored I am to be here, how grateful and humbled. I'm an old man—I guess that's no secret—and I never thought I'd live to experience a day like this, ever get to meet such nice folks as all you. Your little country, it sure keeps coming up with new surprises for me. Holy God, some of the things I could do without, like sleeping under newspapers, or falling through a cane chair up to my shoulders." My dad pantomimed the fall, which sent the class laughing, Aira most of all. "But really, it's been a month of new thing after new thing for me. *Ayubowan*, *wanacome*; Buddhism, Hinduism; eating with my fingers, smashing open a coconut, seeing a rabbit in the moon. All new to me. And playing felt like new because it's been such a long time: playing in the rain with a couple of little girls, playing right in this room and singing those silly songs.

"Hey, I even wear a sarong now. Imagine that, me in a little skirt! Jimmy gave it to me, and I'm not sure if I should thank him or kick him in the rear." He looked over at me, and then looked deeper. "He sure does love teaching you folks. I suppose you know that but it's something for me to be here and see it. A week ago I saw a young fellow teaching in a pretty tough situation, and, let me tell you, he did miracles. Made learning fun without a book in sight. What you did today, all this singing, all this play, that's what you'll be taking with you, that's how you'll work miracles, too.

"Yep, he's a good one, my Jimmy. The little guy nearly shriveled up in my hand but, hey, here he is. He's a teacher, that's for sure, and I guess we're pretty proud of him. Guess we'll keep him." He looked at his watch. "Well, must be time to let you good folks head on home. Sorry if I took up too much of your time. Let me just end by saying—and 'scuse me if I say it wrong—ayubowan. And wanacome."

In the stillness of the room before the applause—first Aira, then the entire class—I could feel my entire body rising and being magnetically pulled toward my dad. There was no sweat on his forehead to dry, no flies on his nose to shoo away. But I touched him anyway, my fingers on the cheek of my dear old dad.

It didn't startle him, this touch.

Bananas, a small Buddha, mangoes, a picture book of Sri Lanka, avocados, a sack of rice—my father was presented with so many gifts as he left the DELIC that we had to leave most of it behind in the office for another day. When no student was watching, Aira handed my dad an aralia flower and then trotted away with Gita by her side. We walked with the students until the fork in the road, and then watched them wave and cheer and twirl a few final hokey-pokeys before we turned our backs and headed home.

"Sir. One moment, sir." It was Kamalendren, breaking from the pack of students and pulling something out of his pocket. "Please, sir. Please accept this simple gift. My son, he makes it himself, and he asks me to give it to you." He handed my father a miniature wooden elephant painted in gaudy colors. "It is for good luck, sir."

My dad turned the elephant over in his palm, awed as if holding a rare jewel, and then slid it into his pocket to rest alongside the chipped Buddha and rosary. "And for your son," he said, "please pass this along to remember us silly white folks."

Kamalendren accepted the gift with a deep bow, clutching Big Green to his chest as if it were a life.

We walked alone downhill toward our house. The last light of dusk cast our bodies into long shadows that stretched out before us. The dying of daylight marked the beginning of firelight, and in each of the homes we passed along the way we could see and hear the circle of life around the hearth: a grandfather snapping twigs, a mother cleaning rice, a son whacking open a coconut. We looked upward to see hundreds of glowworms sparkling like starlight in the branches overhanging the road. My dad stopped to admire them, and as he did he sighed, "Ahhh." And again, "Ahhh." For a long while he just stared at the worms and at the stars behind them. Then, whispering so softly that I nearly missed it, he said to himself, "Don't forget it. Don't ever forget to look up."

And I looked up at the Big Dipper, overwhelmed nearly to tears that I had lived to see this day: my dad playing with me, singing with me, seeing me. I had lived to touch his cheek, a sweet and holy sensation now forever in my fingertips. Once again I linked arms with him and drew him close, and together we marveled at the twinkling wormlight that brought to life the night sky, our only sounds the sounds of "oooooooh" when falling worms and meteors would flash across the black.

A shutter squeaked. We remained hypnotized by the night until the shutter squeaked again, now more insistent. It's mute Nishanka, I thought, up to her old games. She wasn't at the window, but there in the line of our sight at the base of the avocado tree leaned a brown paper parcel. I picked it up.

The paper was warm in my palms. The three of us encircled it, drawing closer to inhale its sweet scent. Cindy untied its crude string

195

and there inside, huddled together, were three buns crusted on top with sugar and coated on the bottom with ash. Cindy and I knew this was more than food I held in my hands.

"Looks like an invitation," Cindy said. "I think it's time we answered it."

We walked up the path to Nishanka's mud home. This was our first visit, though we had passed this house daily on our way to DELIC, hearing the squeak of the shutter and glimpsing at times a retreating, shadowy figure. We knew her name to be Nishanka, though Amma referred to her as either *yaka* (devil) or *bala* (dog). Amma often warned Cindy that if she were pregnant, one look at Nishanka would immediately strike the fetus mute. Cindy's response—*And what about you? Would one look at you turn a fetus into a thief?*—usually sent Amma away in a huff.

Nishanka was mute because, at age six, she fell out of a truck while helping her father deliver bread. As with many disabled Sri Lankans, Nishanka was then banished indoors forever, never to learn sign language, never to swing upside-down from mango trees. She watched the passing of others' lives through her bedroom shutters, her only words the squeak of a rusty hinge. Usually she just baked bread all day with her father in a dim, smoky kitchen behind the house; he then delivered the bread throughout the neighborhood from the only vehicle he would ever ride again: a bicycle.

On this night, Nishanka's mother greeted us at the door with a deep bow. She was expecting us, she said, and then led us to the three chairs resting in the center of the room, lit golden by the candles and oil lamps. She sat on the floor in front of our feet, looking up. I could see from the deep wrinkles of her face that her life had not been easy.

After a short while the mother turned her attention to a back room, calling, "Nishanka. Endewa, endewa." I followed the line of her mother's sight and there, clinging to the shadows of the doorway, was Nishanka, phantomlike in her white sari. With her mother's encouragement she stepped partially into the light, retreated, then walked rapidly toward us with her head bowed so low that I couldn't see her face. She dropped to her knees in front of my father and awaited his touch.

What did this mean to her, this touch from an old white man? Or from this younger man she had spied walking past her house for two years? I watched her closely to read the language of her muscles, half-expecting her to faint or at least to sigh "Ahhh" over and over.

But it didn't happen. I noticed many things about her—patches of flour on her arm, coconut-oil stains on her sari, fingernails bit to the nub—but what I noticed most of all was that she wanted to get away from us men.

It was to the woman she inclined. When she had positioned herself in front of Cindy, Nishanka bowed a very slow ceremonial bow. Her forehead came to rest on Cindy's feet, and at that moment of skin meeting skin, of both women inhaling deeply and staying locked in that position, I knew that this was no place for men. Woman to woman, warmth to warmth, there was a power created in that contact that was a stranger to me, a power that reached back ten thousand years and circled the globe. For all I knew the earth may have stopped revolving, then resumed once Nishanka's shoulders began to tremble. She was crying. Cindy cupped her hands around the sides of Nishanka's face and tilted her head upwards until their eyes met.

"Ayubowan, Nishanka," Cindy said. She wiped the tears from Nishanka's cheeks with her thumbs and repeated, "Ayubowan."

This was no mere word, just as my father's *wanacome* to the Tamils was no mere word, either. This *ayubowan* had fingers, reaching down deep and deeper still into the most human of places within this deaf woman, that ancient place that is all about being noticed. I had felt it a few hours earlier at DELIC when my dad said, "I guess we're pretty proud of you, Jimmy," and I could feel it in that home when Nishanka mouthed her silent, "Ayubowan, Miss Cindy." That silence overwhelmed me like a scream.

*Ayubowan.* The god in Cindy had met the god in Nishanka, speaking in a language more advanced than words. Their eyes found yet a deeper place in which to look, and it scared me, the intensity of that stare. If I had put my hand between the line of their sight, that stare would have burned a hole right through my palm. And I knew, matter-of-factly, that during our three years together this wife of mine had never gazed at me with a fraction of that intensity, and never would.

The night continued with Nishanka on the ground leaning against Cindy, their fingers interlaced. They listened to my dad answering the mother's questions about life in America. He showed the pictures he carried in his wallet. "This one, this here is Lil and me, about 1950, on the Atlantic City boardwalk. Oh, and this here's me in my judge's robes, and that's the Cleveland skyline behind me. Last one, this here's the kids next to a snowman they built."

Nishanka and her mother understood none of this. Snowmen, skyscrapers, boardwalks? The other contents of my dad's wallet baffled them even more: credit card, insurance card, library card, driver's license. We tried to explain the concepts behind them—for example, how the ATM card gets money out of a wall—but there was no sense to be made of this wallet-full of riddles. My dad sighed at the trouble of cramming all the cards back in place, and I wondered if that sigh was also for the absurdity of these cards: vital in America, useless and even comical in Sri Lanka. The speed and protection behind each card was just a thin cultural oddity, and by the way my dad slapped shut his wallet, I think he may have realized this, too.

Suddenly Nishanka stood and rushed to a back room. I was alarmed that maybe we had insulted her in some way, but just as quickly as she had left, she returned, carrying a platter of twenty freshly baked cookies.

198

*You must take them all,* her mother insisted. *Nishanka makes the best cookies in all Bandarawela.*

I said we'd take a few.

*You'll take them all! And tomorrow you come back for more. Isn't that right, Nishanka?* Her mother gesticulated this message to her daughter. Nishanka nodded her head emphatically and flashed her fingers. *Forty. Nishanka says you get forty tomorrow and . . .*—more hand flashes—*fifty the day after.*

Soon our laps were filled with pretzel sticks and buns and doughnuts. *Nishanka is proud of her doughnuts,* the mother said. *Finish these and we will send more to America.*

When the mother handed us five loaves of bread, we said that enough was enough and that we couldn't possibly eat all of this food. *Then give what is left,* she said, *to Mudalali and Amma. Just remember that before you do, add a secret ingredient.* She drew us close and whispered like conspirators. *Be sure to add a stone or two in the middle.*

The joke surprised me. While we laughed, the mother pantomimed for Nishanka the insertion of rocks into Amma's bread. Cindy then pretended to be Amma, chomping down on the stone in the bread and then spitting out her one broken tooth. Nishanka silently laughed along with us. My father got into the act by being Mudalali, one hand rubbing an exaggerated belly, the other hand dragging on the ground like an orangutan from the weight of an imaginary ring.

We laughed at the theatrics but we were really laughing from the sweetness and the community of this scene. Soon we all noticed by the changed pitch of that laughter that someone else in the room was also amused. It was Nishanka's father. He was leaning against the door to the kitchen wearing an apron, his hair dusted with flour, his arms and legs chiseled into sinew from a lifetime of labor. He stepped forward into our room and raised his hand. *After Mudalali eats the bread with the stone,* he said deeply, *I wonder which of his toilets will receive the little gift.*

Our heads shot back with laughter, and our laughter grew and grew. As the mother squatted to mime for Nishanka the image of a fat Mudalali suspended over a toilet, that wild laughter elevated to another level, to the kind of laughter so extreme that there is no sound, the six of us in that golden flickering candlelight all struck mute by joy.

# II

His first good-byes were to the house. Barefoot and wearing a sarong, my dad touched the walls and a gecko's tail before stepping outside to run his fingers through the rainwater in the cistern. He watched a trail of ants streaming across the kitchen floor and up a table leg. On the table was the coconut hatchet, which he lifted and lowered in a slow-motion split of an imaginary coconut. On the way into his bedroom he stopped for a moment at the Buddha shrine, straightened the aralia flower from Aira that he had placed there yesterday, then bowed. I leaned into the room.

"We need to get going, Dad," I said softly.

He rose from his bow. "Going? What for?"

"We just need to get going."

In the bedroom it took some time for him to change into his wool pants. He ran his fingers down the length of his sarong before unhitching it at the waist, letting it fall in a heap around his ankles. He folded it ceremoniously into tight squares, like a flag, and then stepped into his wool pants. Into one pocket he placed his rosary and elephant and Buddha; into the other went his wallet, thick with credit cards and nearly all the rupees from his first day. He had spent only $250 or so of the $2,000 he brought with him, and that included a sapphire.

"C'mon, Dad. Our ride will be here any minute."

"I'm coming, I'm coming."

In a few minutes he stood in the front doorway, slipping his dung-soled feet into his wing tips. He closed the door behind him. It would probably be the last door he would close for a long time that had no lock. Keys awaited him, and I wondered which would be the first to be emptied from his pockets back in Cleveland: some of his keys or the chipped Buddha statue.

Outside, Amma insisted that we eat breakfast at her grand table. We said no, she said yes, and this went back and forth until Amma gave up and asked my dad for his watch.

We waited for the Peace Corps jeep in front of our house. By chance it was up in this area delivering books to a nearby orphanage and could take us straight to Colombo. I thought this arrangement would thrill my dad, this exchange of twelve hours standing on a packed and steaming bus for five hours in air-conditioned, padded comfort.

"I vote for the bus," he said. "As long as we have time I don't see why we—"

"Dad, don't be ridiculous. You *never* pass up the jeep. That's Peace Corps rule number one. But hey," I joked, "you can always take the bus on your own and we'll meet you in Colombo."

He asked if that was possible.

I turned from him and searched the bend in the road for the jeep. In the meantime the characters of Bandarawela passed us one by one: the cricket team, the turbaned man blowing snot at our feet, the cross-eyed twins. My dad asked me for a pen and wrote "eye doctor, get patches" on his palm. He looked up at the sound of a bell. It was Nishanka's father on his bicycle delivering loaves of bread. He threw a fresh, warm loaf into my hands without stopping or saying a word.

An elephant loped by, the cow in high heels swaggered by. A gypsy in a bullock cart urged us to buy a pot. A boy with a flute stopped to enchant a cobra out of his basket—for ten rupees. I searched again for the jeep and saw instead a garish turquoise car approaching us.

It was Mudalali's car. In his infinite lunacy he was driving past us over and over, first a hundred yards forward then a hundred yards back, again and again. Our eyes followed his car like a very slow tennis match until I felt something hit my calf. I looked down. It was a papaya, and then a mango, and then three bananas—all thrown from a nearby bush. When Mudalali stopped up the hill to put his car in reverse, we heard a rustle in the bushes and then saw Shamila, still wearing her one tired dress, darting out onto the road and running in her bare feet as fast as she could, far, far away.

I loved the Peace Corps jeep. I loved the thick upholstered seats, the power locks and electric windows, the cup holders and the dome lights. I especially loved the air conditioning, which Amma felt and then jumped back, saying something about the devil.

This was my own little America, insulated and full of excess. As if sensing exactly that, my dad stood outside his front door and scanned for one last time this world of Bandarawela: the banana trees, the panorama of blue and hazy mountains, the many black faces smiling broadly. He looked up to Nishanka's house on the hill, and there she was, leaning out the window into the morning light and waving wildly. This was the first time many of her neighbors had ever seen her, and they joined with my dad, calling, "Ayubowan, Nishanka!"

From inside the jeep I reached out and tugged on his shirt. "Let's go, Dad. The driver has to get going."

After more waves and more *ayubowans* he slipped into the jeep and shut the door tight, its suction sound reminding me of a refrigerator. The jeep inched through the dense crowd, blaring the horn. My dad turned the air-conditioning vent away from his face and looked out his window, that thin membrane now separating climates, sounds, comforts, skin tones. The villagers, trotting alongside the jeep, had covered the window with the palms of their hands. My dad frantically matched his palm to theirs until one by one they dropped away as the jeep picked up speed and was gone forever.

For the first hour of the ride we said nothing. My father stared out the window, admiring for the last time in his life the rice terraces and parrots, the chalk-white Buddhist temples, the elephants sauntering in the streets without anyone taking notice. After a while he asked me about the grove of trees with their barks slashed with diagonal strips.

"Those are rubber trees," I said.

"Rubber trees?"

"That's right. Rubber trees."

"Never seen a rubber tree before."

And then silence for another hour. At one point the driver pulled over at a famous and spectacular waterfall, assuming we would want to hike up close to the lookout. But Cindy was asleep and my dad was murmuring his rosary and I was too fond of the air conditioning to step outside. The driver shrugged and pulled back onto the road. Before speeding away, though, I caught a quick glance of a couple cradling two limp dogs that had most likely just suffocated to death in their parked car.

An hour later I broke the silence with a question. "Would any of you ever give mouth-to-mouth to a dog?" No one answered, and when I asked it again, Cindy opened her eyes just enough to look at me with contempt. She then turned her back to me and fell asleep against her window.

She slept through a checkpoint. I handed her passport to the teenage soldier, his rifle pointed nonchalantly at the driver's head. Behind him were other soldiers ushering a crowd of people off a bus. Part of me wanted to be smothered among them, to be part of the world's vast majority who rely on these ragged buses to get around. The other part of me asked the driver to turn up the air conditioning. It was this other part that snarled at the bus passenger who yelled something vile at us, and so when a soldier knocked him to his knees with the butt end of his rifle, I felt a smug satisfaction that the fellow got what he deserved.

What was happening here? I tried to make sense of it all but my head hurt. We entered the outskirts of Colombo and my head hurt more. We drove through deep potholes and passed communities sheltered beneath cardboard lean-tos. Where were the tea fields, or Saturn, or the Hokey-Pokey now? With each mile the smog and the traffic and the overall bedlam grew thicker. Tires burned in columns by the roadside. Idle soldiers threw stones at a cardboard Kodak model strung from a tree. When the traffic forced the jeep to a crawl, faces stared in at us. Some hissed.

At one point we came to a long halt at the same traffic signal we had stopped at a month earlier. Up above, Rambo and V. J. Kuma-ratunga still loomed over the city, and all around were the same blaring horns that vibrated the sides of the jeep. I turned to the tap at my window, and there stood the same beggar woman with the same crusty baby at her breast, looking desperate as ever. I opened my electric window a crack and let a five-rupee coin fall on the asphalt, then sealed my window up tight. I settled back in my seat and took hold of Cindy's hand. But she didn't hold back, and every muscle in my hand knew it.

The jeep dropped us off at the Lake House. The plan was to check in, go over and eat at the Hilton, then just lounge around the next day by the pool until my dad's evening flight. As soon as the jeep pulled away, however, I knew the plan had problems.

There was no Fez to greet us. In fact, there was no one to greet us, and as we approached the entrance we realized that the Lake House was deserted. The automatic sliding door was full of bullet holes and off its track; the letters of the sign "Lake House" were charred and melted. I stood on broken glass and peered in between the bullet holes, and saw that the lobby was wrecked and looted. No tiles, no chandelier, no fountain. Without looking at each other, we said empty words—"what a shame," "when did this happen," "JVP's getting serious"—and decided to go eat at the Hilton.

To get there we had to cross Galle Road, packed as always with buses and trishaws and army tanks and whole families on bicycles. We leaned into the traffic for our moment to sprint across. Like squirrels, we darted and stopped and retreated, darted again and hesitated, and then finally, in a terrified bolt, made it across.

The doorman at the Hilton shook free the few beggars we had attracted along the way. He escorted us to the restaurant, using such Fez-like words as "inestimable" and "cater to your whim" and "boundless ecstasy." And sure enough, I did feel some boundless ecstasy: I wanted a fat old steak, my first in two years, and this was the best place for it. My dad was doing his dadly duty by springing for the most expensive dinner on the island for us tonight. At first the idea thrilled me—linen napkins! heavy forks! beef, beef, beef!—until we stepped into the restaurant.

Every table was empty. Against the wall stood twenty idle waiters, all in tuxedos, all a little bit stunned to see actual customers. Three of them stepped forward to pull out our three upholstered chairs. Three others brought us ice water and French bread and a wine list covered in velvet. The three dinner menus, brought to us by three new waiters, were also covered in velvet. I opened mine. The prices were in dollars, and I quickly calculated that tonight's meal and drinks could cost my dad somewhere in the neighborhood of a Sri Lankan's yearly salary: about $280.

My head throbbed. Somewhere outside of that dull ache our waiter was rhapsodizing about "garlic escargot" and "orange vinaigrette" and "your chef, Wolfgang." Somewhere beyond that were the notes of a piano. It was a polished Steinway grand, its shiny lid propped open like a coffin, being played by a man in a tuxedo with much too big of a grin.

All of a sudden I pushed away from the table. "I have to go," I said, rubbing my temples. "I have to go now or I'll scream."

A waiter from nowhere rushed to pull out my chair. I glared at him and he backed away into a corner. I stood up, toppling over my chair, and stormed past all the vacant tables and idle waiters until I pushed open the brass door as if I'd been underwater and running out of breath.

Outside I sucked deep the squalid city air and sat, alone, on the edge of a curb. I didn't know why this massive funk was overpowering me, but it was, and the best I could do was keep my feet from being run over by buses. Beggars left me alone. Pigeons left me alone. I buried my head in my arms and breathed deep.

"Do you know where a guy can get a good wadee around here?"

I looked up. There stood my dad and Cindy, both smiling and both insisting that it was never their idea to splurge for a Hilton steak. They thought it was my idea, my need, and they were right. The throb in my skull immediately took flight. Suddenly my only concern was to tell my dad about the green thing stuck between his teeth. He sucked hard but it stayed put.

"Come here," I said, waving him down.

He bared his teeth at me and held out his arms as if parachuting down on top of my head. I told him "hold still, hold still," and with the concentration of an engraver I dug away. All that mattered to me at that moment—not the air-conditioned jeep, not the velvet wine list—was my dad's dental hygiene. The complexity of life was now no more than a fingernail on a tooth. And as I held up my fingernail to my dad and declared in triumph, "I got it! See, I got it!" I knew that what I really "got" was the insight that the darkest of funks can metamorphose into love with the ease of a simple touch.

A bus braked inches from my toes. I looked above the windshield to the destination and read in swirling Sinhalese letters, "Hikkaduwa," a beach resort an hour to the south. I jumped to my feet. If ever I knew I was in the presence of serendipity here on the isle of Serendib, it was now.

"Let's go," I said, gathering up our bags. "Let's go for a swim."

The bus was gloriously overcrowded. It smelled of curry and chickens and bodies that had worked all day. A woman in a seat opened her arms as an offering to hold our bags. A man next to me insisted I take a few wadees from his greasy paper cone. I held one out to my father.

"Hey, Dad, you up for a wadee?"

He snatched it out of my hand. "Been waiting all day for one of these," he said.

Eventually a window seat opened up for him. For the rest of the journey he leaned his head out the window like a dog in a pickup, smiling into the wind.

We arrived at Hikkaduwa at dusk. The long line of taxis wrapped around the block, and when we, the only tourists on the last bus of the night, entered the first cab, all the others drove away, probably home. The nighttime curfew would soon be in effect, ending what little business these cabbies had had all day in this deserted tourist town.

The owner of the little motel did not come out to greet us. He hid behind the front desk, sure that anyone out at this hour could only mean trouble. When he heard Cindy speak Sinhala, he slowly rose up, staring in disbelief at white tourists speaking his language. It took him a while to find the registration book; when he opened it, the binding cracked like stiff knuckles. The last tourist listed in the registration book was Steffan Damek, signed four weeks earlier. As we paid the three dollars for the two rooms, I could feel the suspicion in the owner's stare, and when his small son ran out to greet us, the boy was ordered sharply to get back in his room.

We stood on the balcony. Somewhere out in the blackness rolled the Indian Ocean, but because the curfew applied to the beach as well, all we could do was listen to it from our room. The waves pounded, and so did the explosions not very far away in the JVP stronghold of Weligama. From the balcony I could see the Big Dipper on the horizon, and I was lost in it for a moment until a pair of soldiers, patrolling the beach, saw us and firmly ordered us inside.

For the rest of the evening we sat cross-legged on a bed, playing cards by the light of a kerosene lamp. At one point I stood up to answer the knock at the door. No one was there, but below me on the floor rested a platter of sliced pineapple. When I stooped to pick it up, I saw the heels of the owner's son running away down the hall.

Our pineapple fingers made a mess of the cards. No one minded, least of all me, who was overjoyed to be playing hearts with my dad after such a long time. We used to play it often, especially on vacations at the beach, when my hands were too small to hold all the cards. He never let me win. Never. For a long time it was humiliating to lose so often and so badly, but eventually all that mattered was the joy of just playing with my dad. That's how I felt there in the motel room, the three of us cross-legged in a circle, playing, while not too far away the bombs were at work killing both fathers and sons.

This time I thought I could beat him at hearts for the very first time. In fact, as a full-grown adult with a fully formed brain, I thought I could win with an exclamation: I would take every trick ("shooting the moon," a near impossibility against my dad) and thus shower these two dunderheads with enough penalty points to bury them alive. At first I was sly, casually taking easy trick after easy trick without any alarm. And then, in a flourish, I threw down the ace of hearts and let my intentions be known.

My dad sniffed the air. "Cindy," he said, "do you smell a skunk?"

She sniffed. "Something is sure smelling up the joint."

He sniffed yet again, and in an Irish brogue he said, "Oh, lordy lordy, 'tis a skunk for sure, tat's what it is. Oh Dear Saint Paddy, protect us wee helpless children from the skunk or he'll be makin' taffy out of our limbs tonight. Oh sweet Jasus"—he blessed himself—"the skunk be shootin' for the moon on this blessed night of our Lord. We'd best be stoppin' the lad."

And he did. Three moves later he nailed me with a measly four of hearts, a card I thought had been played already. He laughed with the deep satisfaction of knowing that he could still outwit his son. And I laughed at the symmetry of it all: trounced in hearts as a kid, trounced in hearts as an adult.

The laughter stopped when the door opened without a knock. There stood the owner holding a kerosene lamp, telling us to please dim our light and to please stop talking. I understood his edginess when I saw a soldier standing behind him, a cigarette drooping from his lips, a rifle leveled straight.

The next morning we awoke at daybreak. I ran out onto the balcony and found my father already there, enchanted by the vast white beach and the line of turquoise water.

"The Indian Ocean, Jimmy," he sighed, inhaling deeply. "Who'd ever think I'd live to see the Indian Ocean. First the Sahara, and now this."

I told him that it had been a dream of mine to swim once again in an ocean alongside him, much as we had done a long time ago at Ocean City. "Do you remember that time, Dad?"

"Oh, do I ever. I never saw a kid cry so much in all my life as you on that beach looking up at those big waves."

The owner's wife brought us breakfast without our asking and without any charge. We ate quickly and then changed into our bathing suits—Cindy in the bathroom, my dad right in front of me. While changing, my dad caught his toe in the gauzy inner lining of his suit, twirling him around on one foot in front of me and exposing more than I cared to see.

Out on the beach we spread our towels in the shade of a coconut tree that swung out low and long like an Alpine horn. In one hand my dad held his rosary, in the other a bottle of Coppertone, strength number 45. "Lather me up good, Jimmy. Malone and your mother, they warned me about this sun. Lather me up good or I'll be paying the piper later."

I spread the Coppertone across my dad's freckled and pitted back. The coconut smell, and the lathering, reminded me of those vacations on Lake Erie beaches when the stench of dead fish, belly-up from mercury poisoning, overwhelmed the fragrance of Coppertone.

All lathered, we stood and faced the Indian Ocean. For me it felt like every minute of my life had led to this bright point, to me and my dad ready to swim in the ocean after all these years. Yet how odd: here in the Indian Ocean of all places, here in Sri Lanka of all places. I stood there with my eyes closed, feeling the mystery and majesty in the moment, and then opened my eyes.

"Dad," I said, spreading wide my arms, "I give you the ocean."

And then we ran. Hand in hand in hand the three of us ran across the burning sand and down the damp dark slope and then hopped the little ripple waves until, losing Cindy's grip, I fell with my dad and my dad alone into the embrace of the sea. Together we rose to the surface.

"Bath water!" he cried, rolling onto his back and floating like an otter. "Hot as bath water!"

He closed his eyes and sighed, and in that sigh I knew he had already left the ordinary earth back on shore. Back there were all his troubles—criminals snarling in his courtroom, the decay of his own body, the ordered life of the suburbs—and I wondered if all problems of all lives could be solved out here in the ocean. I pictured the Sri Lankan army and JVP soldiers all afloat, their uniforms and weapons scattered back on the beach. Out here these brutes would soften. Out here they'd forget the old lie that a petty feud was reason enough to ravage their country.

For a while I swam with Cindy. First we pretended we were synchronized swimmers, then we pretended I was knocked overboard from a barge and she swam through rough seas to save me. From there we became sharks and swam toward my floating dad, our hair pushed up into dorsal fins. I added the ominous *Jaws* theme and together we chomped down on him, devouring his head and ripping into his ribs, yet all the while he just kept repeating, "Ahh, this is heaven, kids. This water is heaven."

All he wanted to do was float. The waves wouldn't start swelling for a few hours, so now was prime floating time. Cindy swam away while I held my dad in my arms. I think he fell asleep. I surveyed this body in my arms, this body of an old white man who was borne into Sri Lanka on the emergency chute of a jet. He came with sand on his shoes, I thought, and he'll leave with sand between his toes. I looked at his toes rising above the ocean like an archipelago and thought about how those Cleveland toes now knew the feel of cow manure. And then up to his legs that now knew the feel of a sarong and the feel of a newspaper that keeps off flies. Up to his poor bladder that forced him to face a goat in the night, and to his rump that met his left hand. Up to his heart, now pumping full with others' blood: Rufi, Nishanka, an entire Tamil community, Kamalendren, me. Over to his hands that had held an ancient sickle, and to that finger that let drip a little boy's spit. Up to his ears that heard Benny Goodman in the jungle, over to his eyes that had seen the Rabbit Moon, down to his tongue that made sense out of *wadees*, out to his lips that formed the words *ayubowan* and *wanacome* and *teeka-teeka*. And there in the dead center of it all, his forehead, where a Hindu priest applied a saffron dot and where his youngest son, lifting a mosquito net, reached down to meet that forehead with a kiss.

I released my arms from beneath the body of my father. With his eyes still shut, he floated on his own.

Back on our beach towels, we were not alone for long. A little girl sat in Cindy's lap and asked if she could try on her wedding ring. In my dad's lap sat two little boys, both with bloated bellies and a red tinge to their hair—two sure signs of malnutrition. With great fascination they played with the flap of skin hanging loose like a turkey wattle from his neck. My dad let them jiggle it.

No one sat on my lap. Instead I had to deal with two merchants, one selling perfume, the other selling miniature boats. "Smell smell smell," the perfume man insisted in broken English, "but you beware. One smell and you forever live in Serendib."

The boat man nudged him aside. "I make with my own hand. It float, it cheap, it good. Betty betty cheap. Me boat king. Me king like Reagan."

"Mahatmaya," I said, pushing the balsa boat away from my face, telling him that I just wanted to talk with my dad. "Daeng mama magee paula kataakerannewa, hari da?"

His face exploded in surprise. "Sinhala!" he cried, and I knew I had made a big mistake. "My friend he speak Sinhala!"

But I had not made a mistake. I did speak Sinhala, which was rather amazing, and these men had made boats and perfumes with their own hands—amazing, too. This was their meager livelihood at a time when their children's hair was turning red. I bought two boats, probably the first ones he had sold in weeks, and with it came a fifteen-minute explanation on the intricacies of its construction. The perfume man, meanwhile, uncorked another vial of perfume beneath my dad's nose.

"The smell of love," he said, "the smell of passion. Does sir have wife?"

"Me? Why, sure. Oh, believe you me, my Lil'd love some of this and Malone, he tells me the gals are suckers for this stuff. Lil, she stinks up the bathroom pretty good with all kinds of perfumy things. I'm not so sure of her taste, so whadya say I buy the whole set of them."

A little later all eight of us relaxed beneath the coconut tree. Cindy braided the little girl's hair and the two boys buried my dad's legs in the sand. The two merchants fell asleep close together. And I just stared out to the sea with my dad alongside me, he moving closer and closer until I felt his hand in mine.

"Take it, Jimmy," he said, and without looking I could feel him fold something into my hand. "Go ahead and take it."

I did, and I could feel working its way around my fingers the circle of his treasured Irish rosary.

I just stared out to sea, not quite sure what to say about this first true gift ever from my father. So I just closed my eyes and breathed deep on the salt sea air, feeling the riches in these well-worn rosary beads. Soon I felt a clear directive from this rosary and, acting on it, jumped to my feet.

"C'mon, Dad," I said, offering him my hand. "It's time you and me rode some waves."

The two of us trotted over the hot sand toward the Indian Ocean, the waves looming high and menacing as storm clouds. We held hands. To me, the power of my father's hand could outmuscle the sea. I tightened my hand in his and together, through the sea spray, we ran into the ocean and under the waves. I gulped some salt water and probably whimpered, but as long as my dad sheltered me in the curve of his hand, I didn't care. I was alone with my father in the sway of the sea. We floated for a while and then scouted the waves for one to ride to shore. My dad pointed behind me.

"Watch out, Jimmy. Here comes a doozy."

It was too much of a doozy. Both of us dove under the wave and let it roll over us, a survival trick my dad had taught me long ago at Ocean City. Here on the floor of the Indian Ocean I curled up into a fetal ball, aware that only a few feet away in the same embryonic fluid was my father, curled up, too. In the colossal womb of the earth's ocean my father and I existed as twins, separated in ocean time by the mere blink of forty years.

We floated to the surface. We turned to wait for the perfect wave to ride, and waited, until my dad's eyes grew large.

"Here she comes, Jimmy, and she's a beauty. Oh yeah, that's the one. Now . . . now . . ."—he paddled around in line with the wave—". . . now *ride her!*"

And we did, the two of us kicking our butts up high at just the right time and just the right place, the wave curling white and quiet before it crashed over and around us. I knew what to do. My dad had never taught me how to shoot ducks or how to use a pitching wedge, how to invest money or how to rewire a house. But he taught me everything a boy needed to know about the art of riding waves: butt high, arms straight, exhale slow through the nose and take it up to shore. And so I did, riding this wave so straight and so fast like that man a few feet away—my dad, my teacher of waves. I was all joy inside that wave, and all joy as I rode up onto the beach and scraped my hands against the sand.

I sat up, letting the ocean bubbles wash over me. I looked for my father and there he was, still riding the last push of wave five feet farther up the slope than I could go. He beats me at hearts, he beats me at waves—now and for always. I laughed in my sea of bubbles, watching this seventy-four-year-old man eking out the last inch of wave—like it mattered.

For a while he lay face-down in the shallow surf before laboring to his feet. I watched him stand and then stumble and then stand again, wobbly as a colt. The weight of wet sand in his pockets sagged his swimsuit below the crack of his rump. That crack, that smile, that father—I felt at that moment a love for him as large and immortal as the sea. And I felt a pride in us both: my father, who had answered the mysterious call to fly to Serendib to face his seventh child and his own mob of fears; and a pride in myself, who had honored the duty of all sons to find the elusive way to love one's father.

He walked over to me. He wiped the salt water from his face and, ignoring his drooping suit, stood directly above me as if he were part of the heavens, as if he himself were a celestial body— a Saturn, or an eighth star in the Big Dipper. As he stood there, breathing deeply and slowly, he smiled the purest, youngest smile I'd ever seen on his face, a smile that broke free from the confines of his old skin and floated on air like a feather. Still smiling, he reached down and took hold of my hand.

"Hey, Jimmy," he said, helping me to my feet. "Let's go do that again!"

CPSIA information can be obtained at www.ICGtesting.com
Printed in the USA
LVOW13s1555240713

344448LV00004B/471/P